PRAISE FOR THE BOOK

"*The 8 Cylinders of Success* is a 'literary GPS' for Generation Next. It provides a clear 'trip plan' for the reader via easy-to-follow and useful directions, insights, compelling stories & skill-building exercises. *The 8 Cylinders of Success* shows the reader how to take the most direct route to reach a life filled with inspiration, passion and purpose!"

Kevin Carroll, Author of *Rules of the Red Rubber Ball*, *What's Your Red Rubber Ball?* and *The Red Rubber Ball At Work* & Founder of Kevin Carroll Katalyst consulting agency

"Jullien is a true messenger of purpose, sent to help young people find and live a life of meaning, without waiting for a 'mid-life crisis.' Unlike most books on purpose, *The 8 Cylinders of Success* is filled with practical exercises and tools that will help move you forward along your path. And once you are clearer about your purpose, Jullien will show you how to manifest it!"

Tim Kelley, Author of *True Purpose* & CEO of Transcendent Solutions Consulting

"In this delightful and innovative book, Jullien Gordon writes passionately about how finding purpose can lead to success in business and in life."

William Damon, Author of The Path to Purpose and Director of the Stanford Center on Adolescence and Professor of Education at Stanford University

"Jullien Gordon is so full of wisdom and inspiration. I have learned so much from him, and am constantly amazed at his creative ideas for helping people find purpose and meaning in their lives. Anyone who does all the exercises in this book will benefit tremendously."

Scott Sherman, Executive Director of The Transformative Action Institute

"Jullien Gordon truly is the Purpose Finder. *The 8 Cylinders of Success* is an incredible framework to help any college student find the path to purpose and live a more deliberate and meaningful life."

Steve Loflin, Founder & Executive Director of The National Society of Collegiate Scholars

"Jullien is passionate about enabling others to connect to and fulfill their true life purpose; *The 8 Cylinders of Success* is a guidebook to finding your own path to changing the world."

Ebele Okobi Harris, Director of Business and Human Rights Program at Yahoo!

"This is an enormous undertaking for Jullien Gordon and it will help galvanize the entire country to read and know that the destiny of their future is in their own hands."

Tim Ngubeni, Founder & former Director of the UCLA Community Programs Department

"Jullien's 8 Cylinders of Success gives young people an extremely valuable framework for managing their careers to win – for themselves and for others around them!"

John Rice, Founder of Management Leadership for Tomorrow

"In a world replete with methods of creating plans—business plans, game plans, day plans—Jullien Gordon has offered here a much needed process of determining a primary purpose, upon which plans should be built. Jullien has instinctively and through personal experience recognized that the questions (and answers) concerning purpose are the missing ingredients in happy and fulfilling life. This is a book young (as well as old) should not just read—but use."

Charlie Hess, President of Inferential Focus

"Jullien Gordon speaks to the Millennial Generation in a creative voice that excites and challenges them to act in a directed, purposeful way. Through the 8 Cylinders of Success, Gordon provides a practical and easy-to-follow roadmap for personal and professional fulfillment."

Nicole Lindsay, Executive Director of New York Needs You

THE
X-FACTOR
TO SUCCESS
IS KNOWING
YOUR
WHY

THE

8

TM

CYLINDERS OF

SUCCESS

HOW TO ALIGN YOUR PERSONAL
& PROFESSIONAL PURPOSE

JULLIEN GORDON
FOREWORD BY ANDY CHAN

MVMT
ATTN: Department of Motivated Vehicles
155 Water Street
Brooklyn, NY 11201

For more information about speaking engagements or special discounts for bulk purchase, please contact The Department of Motivated Vehicles at (646) 875-8477 or info@motivatedvehicles.com.

Edited by Lizz Carroll

Designed by Jullien Gordon & Daniel O'Brien

Manufactured in the United States of America

The Library of Congress has catalogued this book as follows:

Gordon, Jullien

The 8 Cylinders of Success: How to Align your Personal & Professional Purpose/Jullien Gordon

ISBN #: 978-0-615-30796-1

20009906901

DEDICATED TO

God, Spirit, Universe, Man-you-fact-urer

My mother for being my motor-vation and #1 fan

Generation "Why"—the Millennial Generation

IN MEMORY OF

Janet Brown: My first writing coach and spiritual editor

Dr. Edward "Chip" Anderson: The StrengthsFinder who led
me to become the PurposeFinder

Angelo Primas Sr.: A small man with big passion and the
father of my best friend

MANY
ACHIEVE A
LOT, BUT
FAIL AT THE
ONE
THING THEY WERE
DESIGNED
TO DO BEST

THE C.E.O. OF YOU

Businesses have visions.
What is yours?

Businesses have strategies.
What are your goals?

Businesses have competitive advantages.
What are your strengths, talents, and gifts?

Businesses have quarterly and annual reports.
How often do you evaluate yourself?

Businesses have operations divisions.
What are your regular processes and routines?

Businesses have research and development divisions.
How do you innovate and creatively express yourself?

Businesses have human resource divisions.
How well do you develop your talent?

Businesses have partnerships.
Who is supporting you?

Businesses have boards of directors.
Who is holding you accountable to your goals?

Businesses position themselves.
Who are you positioning yourself to be?

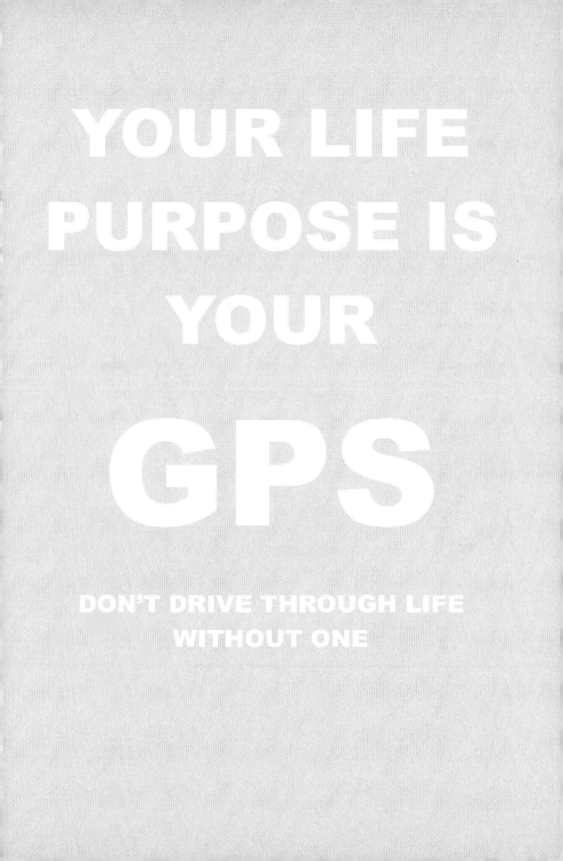

ITINERARY

BEGINNING

PART 1: WHERE AM I?

PART 2: WHERE AM I GOING?

ENDING

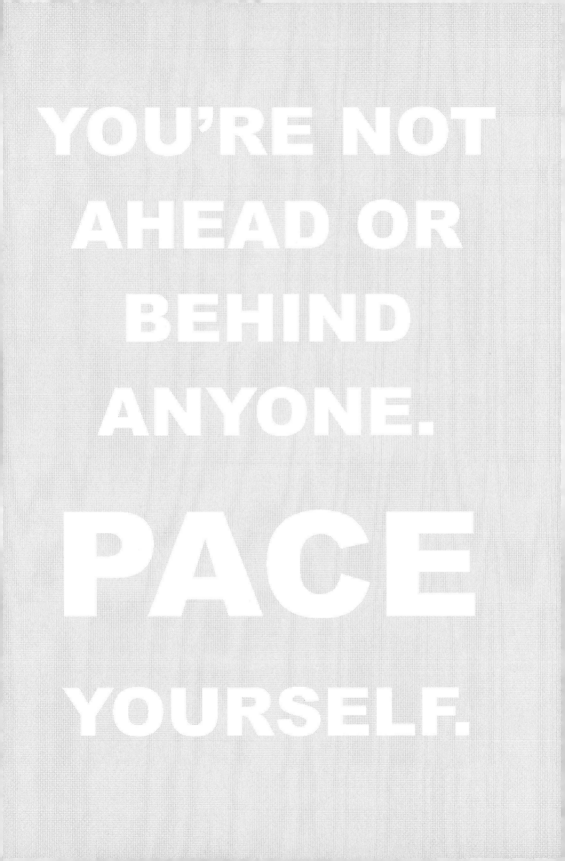

YOU'RE NOT AHEAD OR BEHIND ANYONE.

PACE YOURSELF.

YOUR
CARE-ER
SHOULD BE
SOMETHING
THAT YOU
CARE
ABOUT

FOREWORD

During my tenure as the Assistant Dean and Director of the Career Management Center at the Stanford Graduate School of Business, I taught, mentored and counseled thousands of MBA students and alumni. Some commonly expressed desires among both students and alumni are "I wish that I had more time to reflect on my purpose and vision for my career and life" or "I wish that there was a for-credit class on career and life management." These desires are not unique to MBA students. Wherever you went or are going to school, you're probably asking yourself the same questions right now.

The current reality is that almost all colleges, universities and graduate schools do not see career and vocational development as an essential component of the student's academic career. Most often, the term "job placement" is used to describe the role of the career office, which trivializes the process to just getting a job (or even being "placed" into one) upon graduation. This terminology misleads students into believing that their career paths are finite and diminishes the huge opportunity for soon-to-be graduates to *pave* their own career paths rather than be *placed*. Others use the term "pre-professional school" which communicates that your undergraduate degree is just a stepping-stone to graduate school. Many students choose graduate programs as a default option because they did not spend sufficient time on self-assessment, purpose and vision definition, and generating and evaluating alternatives during their undergraduate experience. Sadly, students who were "placed" in their first jobs or encouraged to go to graduate school later realize that neither path was the appropriate choice and can feel trapped in a path that they do not desire.

Neither the student nor the system is fully at fault. Career development isn't fully embraced by students and career offices nationwide are under-resourced. As I transition into my new role as the Vice President for Career Development at Wake Forest, I am committed to ensuring that students use their academic, extracurricular, and internship experience to position themselves for successful professional careers. In the same way that college should be at the forefront of the mind of a freshman in high school, career should be at forefront of the mind of a freshman in college or first-year graduate student. From there, an undergraduate or graduate student can more fully leverage his or her education to successfully prepare for their 40-year career.

In my 12 years in career development, I have had the opportunity to meet many talented and interesting people. Every so often, I meet someone quite special. Jullien Gordon is one of those unique people. I met Jullien at the end of his second year at Stanford's Graduate School of Business. He and a few classmates organized a special pre-graduation session, called "Reflections," designed to help their classmates reflect on their business school experience in a thoughtful, holistic manner. I was notably impressed when he shared his original poem, The C.E.O. of You (Read it right before the Table of Contents), to several hundred classmates. At that moment, I realized that he and I shared a passion for inspiring people and empowering people to take charge of their lives through defining their purpose, values, passions and vision, and to do so in creative, unconventional, memorable ways.

After a few conversations of sharing our work and our lives, I knew that Jullien and I would be forever linked in our passionate pursuit to bless and serve others in our own unique ways. Wise beyond his years, Jullien conveys his insights and wisdom with passion and creativity. He communicates in an engaging and memorable manner that helps college students, graduate students, young professionals, in fact *anyone*, think more clearly about who they are and where they are going.

In *The 8 Cylinders of Success*, Jullien addresses the big questions every young person asks of him or herself: "Who am I?" "What am I passionate about?" "How do I align my passions with my profession?" "How will I define success?" "What's my vision?" At some point, everyone wrestles with these questions. For many in my generation, it has occurred during a mid-life crisis. For millennials, it is taking place in the "quarter life crisis." These questions are vital to ask oneself at any key transition point in life whether you're going from college to career, career back to graduate school, one job to the next, single to married, career to career, preparing for parenthood, or planning to retire. From my own experience, I can attest that the earlier anyone begins the process of answering these questions, the better off they will be in the long run.

The 8 Cylinders of Success will guide you, your friends, your partner, your child or a colleague to ask and answer all of those questions you wished had been addressed back in college or graduate school. In the book, Jullien describes how he and other notable role models have applied his powerful framework to find and align with their purpose and create a unique vision based on their self-defined metrics of success. As a result, you will be inspired to take the time to self-reflect and to dream in a much bigger way than you ever have before.

Even if you have answered these questions before, it's different every time. Something is new. New experiences. New circumstances. New lessons. New knowledge. New desires. It's a myth to think that you can reflect on your purpose once in your life and then be set forever. Let go of that incorrect assumption and get this book. And then re-read it again when you sense it's time for a tune-up. Before you do your annual New Year's resolutions, look at your notes from doing the exercises. It's pointless to set goals without having clarity on your purpose first. That gets you nowhere fast. Beginning with purpose will make a real difference towards helping you live the purposeful life you've been yearning for.

A common yearning among young adults of all ages is "If only I knew what I wanted to be when I grow up, then I'd pursue it, and *then* I'd be happy." I cringe when I hear this common mantra, because it's become an excuse for many as to why they are not happy. In reality, most people know that:

1. They have no definition for the age of a "grown up"
2. What they want as a career may not provide the lifestyle they want to lead
3. That they might pursue it and not get it, and
4. They're really not certain if following this mantra will truly lead to happiness.

Many use this phrase out of fear that they can't (or won't) figure it out. So, instead of defining and pursuing a job, it's time to first define and pursue your purpose.

The 8 Cylinders of Success is the answer to this commonly used excuse. This enlightening and engaging book is the road map every person needs. On your life journey, you can take the chance of trying to find your way without a road map, but you may pay a steep price by driving off a few cliffs. Why take the risk? Ironically, the biggest risk someone can take in life is *not* pursuing their purpose. This book will redefine who you want to be, what really matters to you, and motivate you to change your life in a new, inspired direction. You will create your own definitions of purpose and success. And as a result, you will discover a deeper fulfillment, satisfaction and joy in your life.

Andy Chan
Vice President of Career Development
Wake Forest University

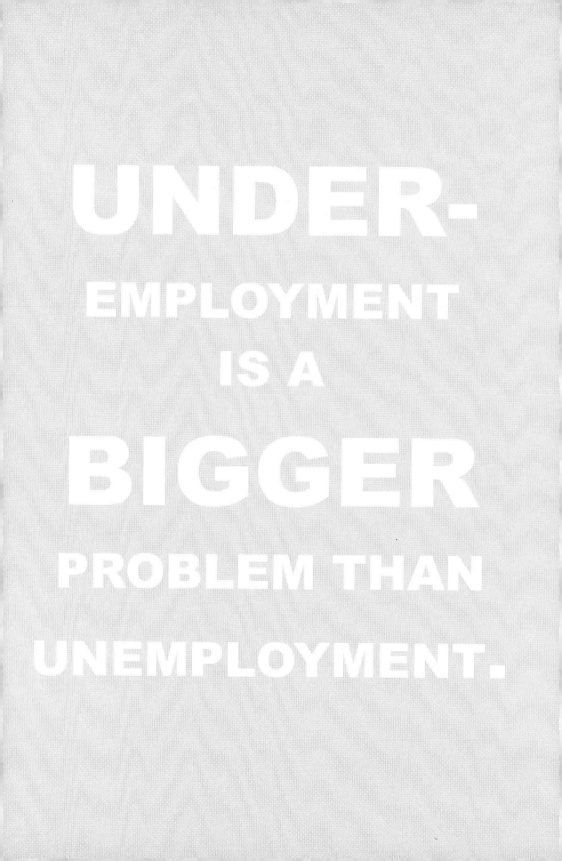

 # PREFACE

THE PURPOSE OF THIS CHAPTER IS TO:

- Identify where you are on the path of purpose
- Introduce you to the 8 Cylinders of Success
- Explain how to use this book to get the best results

QUOTES:

A man who becomes conscious of the responsibility he bears toward a human being who affectionately waits for him, or to an unfinished work, will never be able to throw away his life. He knows the 'why' for his existence, and will be able to bear almost any 'how'."
—Victor Frankl

Quit living as if the purpose of life is to arrive safely at death."
—Mark Batterson

YOUR LIFE IS YOUR VEHICLE

Vehicles drive the entire world. Corporations are vehicles designed to create economic value. Jobs are vehicles to achieve collective visions. People are vehicles to move the world forward. **Your life is your vehicle to design, drive, and maintain. Unfortunately, too many people end up back seat driving through life or driving other people's vehicles and never get in the driver's seat of their own lives.** The purpose of this book is to put you back in the driver's seat of your own life so that you can design the vehicle of your life and achieve your highest personal and professional velocity. **Personal velocity is the speed in which you are able to get to where you want to go. Professional velocity is your ability to close the distance between point A and B for other people and organizations.** You will have renewed your license to live so that you can enjoy the journey of life here and now.

When your personal and professional purpose aren't aligned, you will likely suffer from underemployment. In short, you are probably underemployed if you have ever said or thought to yourself "I hate my job." **Underemployment is the state of employment where an individual is working below their potential because they aren't passionate about the work or their employer doesn't bring out the best in them by allowing them to play to their strengths.** Underemployment is the greatest challenge in the world today because it affects more people than unemployment.

When you are underemployed, you are less passionate, less productive, and less innovative than someone who is fully employed. A company that find and align people whose personal purpose aligns with their professional purpose will likely outperform a company that simply seeks talent people and tries to shape that talent to serve its needs. Underemployment hurts the employee, the company, and the customer.

According to a 2004 Age Wave survey of 7,718 American workers, 42% of workers feel burned out, only 33% of workers said they are satisfied with their jobs, only 20% felt very passionate about their jobs, and only 31% believed that their employer inspired the best in them. So imagine that we have a micro economy of 100 people. Let's say that 9 people are unemployed and 33 people are satisfied. That leaves 58 of workers underemployed. Assuming that a worker is only 50% productive when they are underemployed, the 58 workers only produce the value of 29 (=58 x 50%) workers meaning that underemployment is three times more of an issue that unemployment.

Most people try to separate their life and work, but our life is the summation of how we spend our time. Since we spend so much time in our careers, our personal and professional purposes should be one. **Only through aligning our time and mind, along with our purpose and profession, can we experience a meaningful life.** Work is one vehicle you can use to achieve success in life, but your purpose cannot be contained by a job title—it's much bigger than your career.

The purpose of any vehicle is to get an individual or group of individuals from point A to point B. Your life may be a vehicle to move people from learners to thinkers (i.e. teacher). Your job may be a vehicle to move your company from inefficient to efficient (i.e. operations manager). Your company may be a vehicle to move its customers from uninformed to informed (i.e. Google). Knowing what type of vehicle you have and want to create will help you navigate the journey of life much easier.

We live life like we treat our cars. Our car is an extension of us in many ways. Most people only take their car to the mechanic when something is wrong. Some people believe that it is cheaper to wait until something breaks than it is to take their car in for regular maintenance. Since the full workings of our cars aren't visible or understood, we're unconscious that the wear and tear of one part increases the dependency and strain on others, and thus speeds up the wear and tear of the car as a whole. **The saying, "If it ain't broke, don't fix it" has cost people more in time and money than it has saved them on their cars and their lives.** Some of us are born with "lemons" for lives and some of us are born with "luxury" vehicles. Regardless of what type of life you began with, it will need maintenance.

The word "mechanics" has two definitions: 1. people who repair and maintain machinery, motors, etc. and 2. the scientific study of motion and force. Thus, auto mechanics study the various parts of vehicles so they can ensure that the vehicle can move at its highest velocity. Through this book, we will examine your **mechanics (skills and the patterns and routines that optimize your vehicle)** to improve how you are currently moving in the world and find your highest personal and professional velocity. You will come away with a simple framework that allows you to perform regular maintenance on your life so that you can easily move toward the achievement of your goals faster, safer, and happier with the least friction possible.

As an upperclassman in high school, you may recall going to driving school to get your permit and ultimately, your driver's license. For many people, this was a liberating moment because it meant that you could go places on your own without relying on other people, especially your parents. You had the power to chart your own course, your own day, and your own destination.

The 8 Cylinders of Success™ is a similar process designed to liberate you to live the life you want to live—rather than the life you think you have to live. **The life you think you have to live usually starts with other people's opinions. The life you want to live starts with you.** Sometimes parents try to live vicariously through us, especially if they gave up on their dream. They act like **an officer, people who want the security of office life for you over a-line-meant (a state when all of your 8 Cylinders are harmoniously working together for good)** with your purpose. If these are your parents, it's up to you to navigate their potential traps and radars.

The journey you are about to embark on is all about you. The journey of life is a metaphor used by many throughout history to explain the inner evolution of every human being. Some familiar quotes include:

The journey of a thousand miles begins with one step."
— Unknown

"The journey is the reward."
— Chinese Proverb

"The longest journey of any person is the journey inward."
— Dag Hammarskjold

You are going on a journey within yourself to align the key parts of your life with your passions and purpose so that you can move through the world as powerfully as possible. This book will redefine what it means to be "street smart". "Street smart" is a term often used juxtapose to "book smart" to convey one's level of common sense and understanding of life regardless of their level of formal education. It's great to be "book smart," but formal education only measures your GPA, whereas street smarts measures your GPS or alignment with your purpose. There a millions of people who are extremely "book smart" that could move more powerfully through the world if they developed their "street smarts." When you complete this book, you will have:

- More clarity on your life's purpose and direction and be able to articulate it
- Insights on how to align your passions with your current profession or a new one
- A plan of action to turn your passions into skills that people and companies value
- A powerful vision for your life to motivate you and others

The pursuit of purpose is a self-discovery process. To dis-cover means that whatever you're looking for is already within you—it's just covered up. When designing vehicles, car manufacturers start with a brown block of clay and then they chisel away at it to shape the model car. The car is already in the block of clay in the mind of the designer. No clay needs to be added to the block. Nothing is missing. The designer's goal is to shed the unnecessary clay to reveal the car within in its finished form. **Like the car, you are already whole and complete in the divine mind of your Man-you-fact-urer (the source that you believe is**

responsible for your creation) and this process is designed to expose your true design. Doing so will allow you to end your *search* for purpose and begin your *pursuit* of purpose.

5 POINTS ON THE PATH OF PURPOSE

One day I saw a cartoon of a family on a road trip with the nagging son in the backseat incessantly asking, "Are we there yet? Are we there yet? Are we there yet?" every two minutes. The father finally gets fed up and responds, "Stop asking if we're there yet. We're nomads for crying out loud. As long as we're on the journey we're there."

For the beginning purposeseekers who just want to get there, there is no "there." The pursuit is endless and you can't cut corners. The purposeseeker's journey is always evolving and unfolding into new chapters and directions. Therefore, because there is no "there," it is impossible to compare two people by their proximity to "there." Regardless of age, income, ethnicity, or education, no one is actually ahead of another person because everyone has his or her own path to travel. **Similar to the phrase written on the passenger side mirror of cars, sometimes our *objectives are closer than they appear*. You may be closer to where you want to be than you think, but when you don't have a process to evaluate where you are in relationship to your desired destine-nation (your unique end goal, state, or place), you default to feeling lost or behind.**

As pursuing one's purpose has no predetermined path, many people think that the pursuit is risky. Don't be fooled—it is. **However, pursuing one's purpose is not nearly as risky as choosing not to pursue it at all. By neglecting**

our purpose for various forms of security, we ultimately risk our true happiness and fulfillment. In trying to be someone you aren't, you end up competing with people who are clear on their purpose. That's a game you can't win. The journey never ends, however, the search can. Someone on the path of purpose can move confidently in the direction of their dreams, whereas a person off their path moves cautiously in seek of security.

Purpose is not a destination—You will never say, "I have fulfilled my purpose." Living in alignment with purpose is something we must choose as a way of life in every moment. We are either on the path of purpose (not the path to purpose) or indifferent and off of the path of purpose. On the journey of life we begin off the path of purpose and life supports us in getting on the path through our experiences. There are 5 points on the path of purpose that you can use to define where you are on your journey. The cycle begins internally with one's self and then expands to touch others. These 5 points on the path of purpose are as follows: inquiring, investigating, invoking, investing, and inspiring. The cycle could take someone a lifetime to complete while another person may go through the cycle three or more times sequentially or simultaneously.

Invoke and vocation share the same root word, invocare, which means to call. The more specific your call, the better your answers. This book will help you get through point three, which is invoking, by helping you clarify your purpose statement so that you can voice it to people who support you. Even if you feel like you're already investing or inspiring, this process may confirm, sharpen, or uproot what you're currently doing. **Once you are able to articulate**

your authentic purpose to yourself and others, you will begin to attract the right people, information, and opportunities in your life. The momentum generated from your authentic action and pursuit will carry you forward through points four and five on the Path of Purpose.

5 POINTS ON THE PATH OF PURPOSE

INDIFFERENT
OFF THE PATH OF PURPOSE

5. INSPIRING
STARTING TO INSPIRE OTHERS WITH IT

1. INQUIRING
STARTING TO QUESTION IT

4. INVESTING
STARTING TO PUT ENERGY INTO IT
(I.E. TIME & MONEY)

2. INVESTIGATING
STARTING TO EXPLORE IT

3. INVOKING
STARTING TO VOICE IT TO OTHERS

THE 8 CYLINDERS OF SUCCESS

The 8 Cylinders of Success™ is a framework designed to help individuals and organizations identify and align their lives with their purpose. It is based on academic research and the in depth study of some of the world's most

29

successful people and organizations to help individuals like yourself and the organizations you work for or with discover and align their lives with their purpose. **Your purpose is your personal GPS system that continuously guides you in the right direction throughout life.** Each chapter focuses on one of the 8 Cylinders of Success to help you discover ways to align them and thus create the most powerful vehicle possible from your life. The more cylinders you are able to align, the more powerful your personal movement, but you don't need the perfect a-line-meant of all eight to live a purpose-filled life.

Since we spend so much of our core energy in our careers, it's almost impossible to have a purpose-filled life without having a purpose-filled career. Below you will find charts of the 8 Cylinders of Success for your personal and professional life. Your first goal will be to identify and align your personal 8 Cylinders of Success. Then you will use that information to evaluate how aligned your professional 8 Cylinders of Success are with your personal ones. From there, you will be able to make informed decisions about how you choose to spend your time with your career being one of the most important decisions you will make.

We are all part of one fleet of vehicles. Purpose is the only thing that really differentiates us from each other and makes us unique. And our entire life experience—race, gender, height, family structure, economic class, education level—are all part of the design to help us re-discover that which we know is within us. If you didn't believe it was in you, you wouldn't be reading this book. In order for your purpose to be revealed to you, you have to commit to pursuing it first. Would your parents buy you a car if they weren't sure that you would drive it? To have something and not use it is worse than not having it at all. There is no point in your Man-you-fact-urer revealing your purpose to you if there is a chance you might not live it whole-heartedly. **We must trust that if we were put here for a purpose, then our man-you-fact-urer will provide for us to fulfill it.**

Each chapter begins with a purpose, guiding questions, and quotes related to the chapter's cylinder. From there, I will share an anecdote of someone well known who has embodied the cylinder, in addition to an anecdote explaining how I integrate the cylinder into my life. Within the chapter you will also find a company profile about an organization that embodies the chapter's cylinder and new vocabulary or lane-guage to help you understand the journey. Finally, each chapter concludes with exercises to help you discover and document insights about yourself in reference to the chapter's cylinder as well as a **move-meant (movement with a particular intention)** activity for your personal and professional life to put that cylinder in motion. If you're ready to embark on the journey of a lifetime, then oil your pen, unbuckle your minds, roll down your fears, and start your engine! The journey begins as soon as you turn the corner of this page.

Godspeed!

THE 8 CYLINDERS OF SUCCESS - PERSONAL

Part 1		Where am I?
Principles	Your Dashboard	What beliefs equate to success to me?
Passions	Your Keys	What do I love doing and why?
Problems	Your Fuel	What social, scientific, technical, or personal problem do I want to solve?
People	Your Motor	Who moves you to want to serve them and in what way?
Part 2		Where am I going?
Positioning	Your Lane	What do I want to be #1 in the world at?
Pioneers	Your Pace Cars	Who are my models, mentors, and guides?
Picture	Your Road Map	What's my vision for myself and my world?
Possibility	Your Destination	What's possible in the world *with* me that would not be possible *without* me?

THE 8 CYLINDERS OF SUCCESS - PROFESSIONAL

Part 1		Where are we?
Principles	My Company's Dashboard	What are my company's values and metrics for success? How is my success measured here?
Passions	My Company's Keys	What are my company's competitive advantages and strengths? What strengths am I exercising and developing while at my company?
Problems	My Company's Fuel	What is my company's customers' personal, social, scientific, or technical problem? What related problems do I get to solve?
People	My Company's Motor	Who is my company's target market or customer? Who do I serve to ensure that the end customer receives quality service?
Part 2		Where are we going?
Positioning	My Company's Lane	What business or industry does my company want to establish itself as a leader? What is my career positioning me to be great at doing?
Pioneers	My Company's Pace Cars	Who are the old and new industry leaders? How is my position helping us be an industry leader?
Picture	My Company's Road Map	What's my company's vision for our organization and the world? What's my company's vision for my career?
Possibility	My Company's Destination	What's possible in the world with my company that would not be possible without it? What is or will be possible for my company that wasn't possible before me?

YOUR LIFE
IS YOUR
VEHICLE
TO DESIGN,
DRIVE, &
MAINTAIN

PART 1: WHERE AM I?

In Part 1 we will explore the question "Where am I?" Part 1 is about self-assessment and identifying what is already present within you. **You are perfect as you are right now and every miracle or perceived mistake that has happened in your life has prepared you for what you were put here to do going forward. Everything that has happened in your life has happened for a reason and where you are is exactly where you are supposed to be.** To answer the question "Where am I?" we will begin with the first 4 Cylinders of Success: principles, passions, problems, and people.

YOUR PURPOSE STATEMENT

To document your growth through this process, I ask that you write two purpose statements: an initial purpose statement before going through the 8 Cylinders of Success, and then another statement upon completion. My hope is that the 8 Cylinders of Success will give you clarity on your reason for being so that you can effectively articulate it to yourself and others. **The x-factor to success is knowing your "why" and your purpose statement captures your "why".** The pursuit of purpose never ends, but sometimes we need to take pit stops along the way. By coming to a **S.T.O.P. (stillness to observe patterns)**, you give yourself time to reflect, document, and assess what you're discovering about yourself.

In the legal system, they say, "If it isn't in writing, it isn't legitimate." Written word gives form to your thoughts. Even if you feel that your initial purpose statement isn't right, at least you have a starting point. Write to the best of your ability. Whatever comes to mind arises for a reason. From there you can make adjustments. When it comes to your second purpose statement, I encourage you to write for a different reason. Research shows that when we write something down, we are more committed to doing it than if we simply verbalize or think about it. There will be worksheets to help you clarify your personal and professional answers for each cylinder of success. You will use your answers to craft your final purpose statement at the end of the book.

MY STARTING PURPOSE STATEMENT

Directions: Do your best to write a one to four sentence purpose statement that captures what you think your unique contribution to the world may be.

As of ...., ..., 20..........
          Month   Date   Year

My purpose is to...

....

....

....

....

....

....

....

....

....

....

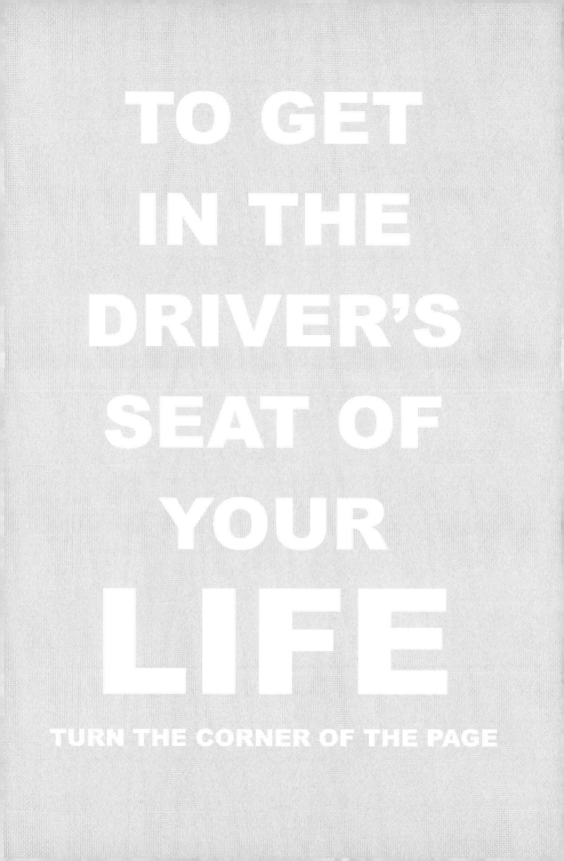

UNBUCKLE
YOUR MIND.
ROLL DOWN
YOUR FEAR.
(LET)
GO

PRINCIPLES »
YOUR DASHBOARD

THE PURPOSE OF THIS CHAPTER IS TO:

- Create a short-term and long-term dashboard for your life and work
- Convert qualitative principles into quantitative measurements

GUIDING QUEST-IONS:

Personal: What beliefs equate to success for me?

Professional: What are my company's values and metrics for success? How is my success measured here?

QUOTES:

The more I have thought about what I believe, the more certain have I become that it is what I have been taught to believe."
— Walter White

Establish unto thyself principles of action; and see that thou ever act according to them. First know that thy principles are just, and then be thou."
— Akenaten

GANDHI'S PRINCIPLE: SATYAGRAHA

Mohandas Gandhi's movement was united by a single principle, *satyagraha*. S*atyagraha* means "the pursuit of truth" and Gandhi believed that life itself was the pursuit of truth. In *Statement to Disorders Inquiry Committee* Gandhi goes on to further define the term:

"I have also called it love-force or soul-force. In the application of satyagraha, I discovered in the earliest stages that pursuit of truth did not admit of violence being inflicted on one's opponent but that he must be weaned from error by patience and compassion. For what appears to be truth to the one may appear to be error to the other. And patience means self-suffering. So the doctrine came to mean vindication of truth, not by infliction of suffering on the opponent, but on oneself."

In "Requisite Qualifications," he goes on to say that, "The *Satyagrahi*'s object is to convert, not to coerce, the wrong-doer." In the face of violence in South Africa and India, Gandhi's redefinition of success as the extent to which the truth was being pursued challenged social norms that were rooted in non-truths. His commitment to truth and the lifestyle that accompanied it led him to become one of the greatest leaders who ever lived.

According to his grandson Arun Gandhi, *satyagraha* wasn't the original principle. Gandhi had to search within himself and among his people to create his philosophy. Arun said that,

"He first called his campaign a civil disobedience but then he gave that up because he said there is nothing disobedient

about what I'm doing. And then he adopted Tolstoy's passive resistance and he gave up that also because he said there is nothing passive about this. It's a very active philosophy."

By way of a community competition, Gandhi's supporters combined two words, *saty* meaning truth and *agraha* meaning the pursuit of, to create *satyagraha*. Old philosophies or the English language could not define Gandhi's movement. He had to create his own definition of who he was and what success in life meant to him.

Out of the singular principle of *satyagraha* came other principles and rules to encourage and help believers know if they were living in a-line-meant with *satyagraha*, but *satyagraha* was ultimately the single most driving force behind Gandhi's thoughts and actions. Gandhi said, "A principle is the expression of perfection, and as imperfect beings like us cannot practice perfection, we devise every moment limits of its compromise in practice." Here he expresses the difficulty of truly living out a single principle every moment and yet, many of us have more than one principle. Living in accordance with our principles is an aspiration, however it is the metric we should use to measure our success without punishing ourselves if we fall short.

Principles are beliefs you can choose to align with in every moment of life. They can be conscious or unconscious, but they are particularly harmful when we are unconscious of what we truly believe. Gandhi said that, "Your beliefs become your thoughts. Your thoughts become your words. Your words become your actions. Your actions become your habits. Your habits become your values. Your values become your destiny." This implies that people determine how they want to be in the world based on their principles first, and then that shapes how they act. Decision always comes before action and we make decisions according to what we believe will lead to our definition of success.

MY PRINCIPLE: THE EARLY BIRD GETS THE WORM

"The early bird gets the worm" is a principle that has directed my life since childhood. Growing up as the child of two doctors, I remember waking up at the crack of dawn to go to school and waiting in the early morning darkness for the first kid to arrive at the playground with a basketball before school. As an anesthesiologist, my mother went to work before the surgery, and as a surgeon, my dad had to be there as soon as the anesthesiologist was done. I deemed them both as successful and their conditioning got embedded in my DNA. It was so ingrained in me that I was even born one month premature. I couldn't wait to take on the world.

Embracing this principle causes me to finish everything early. If I got an assignment at the beginning of the month that was due at the end of the month, I would finish it in the first week while most people waited until the night before to begin. I even finished college early. Once I found out that I could graduate in three years instead of the traditional four, I packed on all of the classes I could handle just to get done early. At every job I've ever had, from working at a batting cage to directing a non-profit, I was always the first in the office by at least an hour. Not only was I more productive during the time when no one else was around, but I also avoided traffic to and from work. I went to business school a few years early as well. Whereas most people begin their

MBA around the age of 28, I finished at the age of 25.

Holding onto this principle also has its downsides. It causes me to be impatient. Sometimes I do things too early or too quickly and I miss out on vital parts of the process or experience. It also means that I'm usually in spaces with older people and sometimes I have to overcome ageism within myself and demonstrate that my voice is equal. All in all, this principle has helped me more than hurt me, so I continue to embrace it today. I love the feeling of waking up early and already having things checked off of my to-do list while the rest of the world is sleeping. It makes me feel focused, ahead, and hardworking. I measure myself by how punctual I am to events and on projects.

PRINCIPLES AS DASHBOARD

Imagine driving a car without a dashboard. You would never know how close your gas tank is to being empty and therefore could get stuck along your journey. You would never know how fast you were going and as a result you may get a costly speeding ticket. You would never know how hot your engine is and the car could overheat causing major mechanical damage that could have easily been avoided. And without an odometer, you could only schedule maintenance based on a period of time rather than miles driven or when something breaks. A dashboard is necessary for any extended journey such as life or careers.

Your car dashboard immediately lets you know how fast you're traveling, how many miles you have traveled, how full your tank is, and how warm your engine is. These indicators help you gauge how successful your journey is moving. Car manufacturers strategically placed these metrics on the dashboard because they believed that these were the four most important metrics for any driver to be aware of at all times. They did not include secondary things like your tire pressure, windshield wiper fluid level or centripetal acceleration. Though important to the car's function, they aren't relevant in every moment. In the same way, your principles co-create the dashboard that allows you to measure your personal formula for success.

Principles shape our relationships with ourselves, other people (i.e. family, friends, colleagues), objects (i.e. information, money), actions (i.e. work, eating), and God. Collectively, one's principles create a way of life that they hold themselves accountable to regardless if they reach their desired destine-nation. **It is possible to get to where you want to be while losing yourself along the way and it is possible to fall short of your destine-nation while staying true to yourself.** Though principles inform our notions of success, being true to ourselves may be a better criterion for success than total distance traveled.

TYPES OF PRINCIPLES

On the journey of life, there are many types of principles:

- Spiritual ("You reap what you sow.")
- Social ("The early bird gets the worm.")
- Financial ("A penny saved is a penny earned.")
- Nutritional ("Food is medicine.").

Principles are the few bumper-sticker-worthy messages that guide our daily decisions—what we will say "yes" to and what we won't. They come in the form of rules, definitions, aphorisms, values, quotes, scriptures, mottos, mantras, slogans, or single words. One principle can be articulated in any of many forms as demonstrated in the chart below. When a principle is deeply engrained in our lives, it usually manifests in a combination of ways.

Principles inform our choices, but they don't make the choices for us. They don't prescribe behavior, they inform behavior: They help us make day-to-day choices, but don't say which choice is right, because in many cases, choice is unlimited. Since choice is unlimited, it would be impossible for any belief system to prescribe how one should act in every situation possible. Two people can believe in the same principle but interpret it in completely different ways. Therefore, it is important to quantify your principles when you can, even if the quantitative measurement

EXAMPLES OF VALUES, RULES, APHORISMS, & POTENTIAL MEASUREMENTS

	PERSONAL	**PROFESSIONAL**
Value	Punctuality	Economic efficiency
Rule	Do not be late	Do not waste
Aphorism	The early bird gets the worm	A penny saved is a penny earned
Potential Measurements	# of times I am early vs. late or # of times I am first to arrive	% reduction in customer acquisition cost or % reduction in variable costs

doesn't capture the full essence of the qualitative meaning. For example, if one of your personal principles is "Do unto others as you would have them do unto you," then you may measure that by the number of random acts of kindness you do for others throughout your day or week.

What gets measured is what gets done. This holds true in life, work and academics. Though the general purpose of education is to equip students with a broad knowledge base, students tend to focus on grades instead of knowledge. Many students employ strategies such as cramming and procrastination to excel on exams and essays without fully engaging the course content. As a result, the moment final exams end, most students forget everything they just learn to pass the test and get the grade.

The exact same mentality gets carried over into our professional lives. At work, what gets measured isn't always explicit. However, through careful observation of whom and how the company culture celebrates success, one can decode the internal dashboard to accelerate their career. Likewise, in our personal lives, constant measurement of our weight, time spent with family, or savings accounts supports us in the achievement of our goals.

THE SOURCE OF OUR PERSONAL PRINCIPLES

Every vehicle has a unique frame and its frame is designed according to its purpose. Some vehicles are designed to achieve high speeds, some vehicles are design to drive off-road, and some vehicles are designed to be comfortable. Our daily choices are made based on principles that we created or adopted over the course of our lives to create our **frame-work (the foundation of beliefs you build your life**

upon). I believe that the purpose of life is a life of purpose. To that end, the 8 Cylinders of Success is a framework I created for myself and others to build our lives upon.

Our principles are typically developed through our environment, experiences, and education. **When you hear someone say, "I made up my mind," it literally means that they built their mind using building blocks of beliefs to arrive at a particular decision.** If you happen to be in a disagreement with them, you cannot change their mind without exploring the building blocks of their beliefs. These beliefs on top of beliefs create the framework for your decisions and life.

Building on top of our frame, we stack on new beliefs until we form our closed belief system that informs us on how we think the world works and how one succeeds in this world. If one piece of our frame causes the vehicle problems, the entire vehicle is put at risk because our beliefs are integrated just like the parts of a car. Therefore, changing one belief, especially a foundational one, requires removing every belief built on top of it. As our principles change, our lives will move in new directions because they create the framework through which we process which choices are right for us.

Principles are typically handed down from one generation to the next through parenting, teaching, and media. You may remember quotes from your childhood that your parents, teachers, religious leaders, or favorite celebrities used to say. These quotes stay with us for years because we have adopted them into our belief system with the only validation being whom it came from rather than testing the aphorism for ourselves. **The challenge with adopting principles from**

previous generations is that the same principles that made one generation successful may not apply to the next generation.

Therefore, it is imperative to be aware of when certain principles are working against us and actually causing mental roadblocks that prevent us from moving forward. **We must measure our integrity by our ability to always act in a-line-meant with our current principles while simultaneously examining if those principles are still valid. This is the process of main-tenets, the inspection of our beliefs or tenets, which are principles held as being true by a person without proof.**

THE IMPORTANCE OF REGULAR MAIN-TENETS

If we maintained ourselves as regularly as we get oil changes, we would have a lot less term-oil (things that cause you to slip during a term or period of life) in our lives. Frequent check-ups are necessary to ensure that we are tuned-up, tuned-in, and aligned with whom we want to be and where we want to go. Public companies are required to evaluate themselves every three months. Along with the daily stock market numbers, their quarterly and annual reports serve as dashboards for management and shareholders to make decisions about the future of the company. Individuals, on the other hand, typically only evaluate themselves once a year, like on their birthday or New Year's Eve.

Regular main-tenets are time periods you set aside for yourself to evaluate your principles so that you can align your time and actions accordingly. **They are like mini re-tire-meants (an opportunity meant to renew yourself and**

your goals like you renew your tires) every day, week, month, or year. Some people participate in daily or weekly spiritual practice for their main-tenets, but sometimes it can be hard to find a mechanism (i.e. church, yoga, meditation, etc.) or mechanic (i.e. executive coach, personal trainer) that you can trust. Mechanics do a full inspection of the vehicle because if any principle is malfunctioning, the vehicle won't work to the best of its ability. Everything must be synchronized in order for you to move at your highest velocity. Your principles co-create your personal formula for success and they can aid or ail you on your journey dependent on how regularly you inspect them.

Like passengers, we pick up and drop off principles along the journey of life. Some people use the term "lemon" to describe a troublesome used car. I have had lemons in the form of cars, but I've also had beliefs that have led to sour experiences in my life as well. When I bought my first car at a used car auction I only evaluated it based on its look and sound. I didn't prioritize the vehicle's working history and upkeep over time. As a result, I ended up paying more money to fix the car than I paid to buy it. **In the same way, we adopt principles because they look and sound good, unaware of the future cost of holding that belief. Like cars, principles need to be test-driven, because principles that sound right can be wrong.** There is no way to be certain up front whether the principles we adopt or create are going to lead us to success and happiness in life, but through regular main-tenets, we can make adjustments until they do.

PERSONAL DASHBOARDS

In our personal lives, rather than just adopting society's definition of success we should create our own metrics and dashboard. Society's definition of success is often limited to material wealth, power, fame, and social status. Through my work, I have discovered that most individuals have their own definition of success, however when it isn't explicit, they tend to adopt society's definition instead. I've experienced people define success by the numbers of lives touched through music, the number of places traveled, the number of lessons learned and shared, the number of ideas turned to reality, and the number of smiles I bring about. Society doesn't celebrate these versions of success through they are unique and important to people.

PERSONAL DASHBOARD EXAMPLE 1

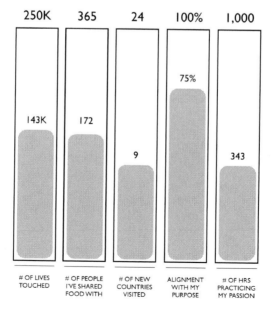

There are so many great quotes and things to believe in the world that it can be hard to identify what truly resonates with you. One way to discover your personal principles is to begin with how you measure success quantitatively and then convert that into a memorable quote. In the worksheet at the end of the chapter, you will use the fill-in-the-blank statements to customize your own frequencies, actions, and measurements for success. You should create three statements and a corresponding quote that represents the principle associated with that measurement of success for you.

Personal Example

You are tired of being late to work and social events. The guy who gets to the office before everyone just got promoted, even though he joined the company after you. This year you decide to be more punctual in all areas of your life because you've noticed that the early bird gets the worm. In order to score how well you're doing, you keep a 3 x 5 index card in your pocket to tally how many times you've been late versus how many times you arrive early.

PERSONAL DASHBOARD EXAMPLE 2

	EARLY vs.	LATE
waking up	₩ ///	//
arrival time	₩ //	//
meetings	///	₩
payment	//	///
bedtime	₩ ////	///

Each day presents multiple opportunities to move the needle on your dashboard. You can measure if you are early or late waking up. You can measure if you are early or late for work. You can measure if you are early or late for meetings throughout the day. You can measure if you are early or late to pay certain bills. And you can measure if you are early or late to go to bed. At the end of each week you can add up your results to measure how punctual you were in that particular week and look for signs of improvement over the course of the month.

PROFESSIONAL DASHBOARDS

Too often companies have lofty values on their websites and in their recruiting materials without a clear indication of how those values are measured on a day-to-day basis. Ideally, companies would recruit, hire, fire, reward, and promote employees based on their principles, however this is rarely the case. In school, your final grade was determined based on exams, homework, and attendance, and you would allocate your time according to the weight of each component. **Just like in school, you must identify how your company and boss measure success for the company, for themselves, and for you.** Your company may have an explicit or discreet rubric for success. If it is explicit, it may be found in the employee handbook, but in most cases it must be observed in the company culture.

The company culture characterizes the interactions between individuals, teams, objects, and information. A cutthroat organizational culture may be characterized by fellow colleagues not sharing vital information in hopes that they will advance ahead of another employee of equal rank. Conversely, a supportive organizational culture may support

COMPANY PROFILE:
PRINCIPLES & ZAPPOS.COM

Zappos.com is an online shoe and clothing company that is gaining national acclaim for its phenomenal company culture. Their company is built on the 3 Cs: Clothing, Customer Service, and Culture. They believe that their culture is the dashboard behind their success so they have metrics in their hiring and performance processes to ensure that it is preserved. They define culture as "committable core values" and their 10 core values are as follows:

1. Deliver WOW Through Service
2. Embrace and Drive Change
3. Create Fun and a Little Weirdness
4. Be Adventurous, Creative, and Open-Minded
5. Pursue Growth and Learning
6. Build Open and Honest Relationships With Communication
7. Build a Positive Team and Family Spirit
8. Do More with Less
9. Be Passionate and Determined
10. Be Humble

Tony Hsieh, Zappos.com's CEO, studies happiness and he finds ways to integrate what he learns into the company culture to ensure his team members' happiness who ensure their customers' happiness which ensures everyone's continued happiness. He believes that in the future, their online customer service model can be leveraged into all kinds of product and service lines, not just shoes and clothes. They project that, "One day, 30% of all retail transactions in the US will be online. People will buy from the company with the best service and the best selection. Zappos.com will be that company." And the core principles stated above position them to be the best in the world in online customer service.

information sharing through cross-functional teamwork and open-door meetings. Those who crack the corporate culture code understand how employees are celebrated and regulated, and thus are able to successfully navigate the corporate ladder.

Who was the closest person to you to get promoted? And why? Who was the closest person to you to get fired? And why? Who among your colleagues tends to have the most freedom and support from management? And why? The answers to these questions will inform you as to what your company truly values despite what the employee handbook or brand book may say. This information can help shape your dashboard so that you can allocate your time in the most productive way possible.

Professional Example

This year's goal for your department is to reduce costs by 10%. Costs have been rising dramatically over the past two years but your manager sees that the competition's costs have remained flat over the same period. Your manager defines these excess costs as "waste" and scolds anyone anytime she sees them wasting anything. In every meeting she always says, "A penny saved is a penny earned," to drive home her point. In order to achieve the goal, you have each of your team members identify their top three cost drivers and develop two strategies to reduce each one. For example, the purchaser may switch to a more cost-efficient supplier and the secretary may order supplies for the year instead of for the month to get bulk discounts. Each week in your team meeting they will share their dashboards. Each dashboard will have the current year-to-date expenses versus last year's and a percent change to quantify success.

At the end of the chapter, you will create your own dashboard and I highly recommend that you share it with your boss to make sure that how you *think* you're being measured and how you're *actually* being measured are aligned. Below is a visual example of a professional dashboard. It will help you make sure that your daily actions are aligned with your weekly and quarterly goals. For your dashboard, choose at least three metrics of success for yourself. Arrange a meeting with your boss and see what they think about your dashboard. Edit the dashboard until you both agree. Post it by your desk and update it regularly.

PROFESSIONAL DASHBOARD EXAMPLE

$250K	250	100	85%	400
			60%	
	172			
$143K				
		35		162
$$$ SALES	# OF SALES	# OF NEW CLIENTS	RETENTION RATE OF EXISTING CLIENTS	# OF NEW LEADS

CONCLUSION

Principles are ideals that define how you want to be in the world. The difference between principles (your dashboard) and purpose (your GPS) is that principles direct decisions that are in line with *who* we want to be, whereas purpose directs our decisions related to *where* we want to be. Car dashboards measure velocity, gas, engine temperature, and distance. And yet, the dashboard of the average car does not gauge the most important measurement on the journey—a-line-meant with our ultimate destine-nation. Knowing that you're driving 70 mph on a full tank of gas doesn't mean that you are driving in the right direction. GPS systems are becoming more standard in cars and hopefully they become more standard in our lives as purpose statements. Though there are many things we can measure on the journey of life like age, income, and number of places traveled, each of us must make sure that our measurements for success are meaningful to us.

Your principles evolve as you experience life. Life's twists and turns will continuously challenge your old beliefs. For many people it is hard to just state their principles off the top of their head, but they are deep inside you informing your every choice. Principles reveal themselves in the midst of tough decisions and situations. **If you haven't challenged yourself, then you probably don't know your true principles and without knowing your principles, it's hard to truly know yourself.** The spiritual search and physical pursuit for one's purpose will be life's greatest challenge and principles will be shed, grown, and shed again along the way.

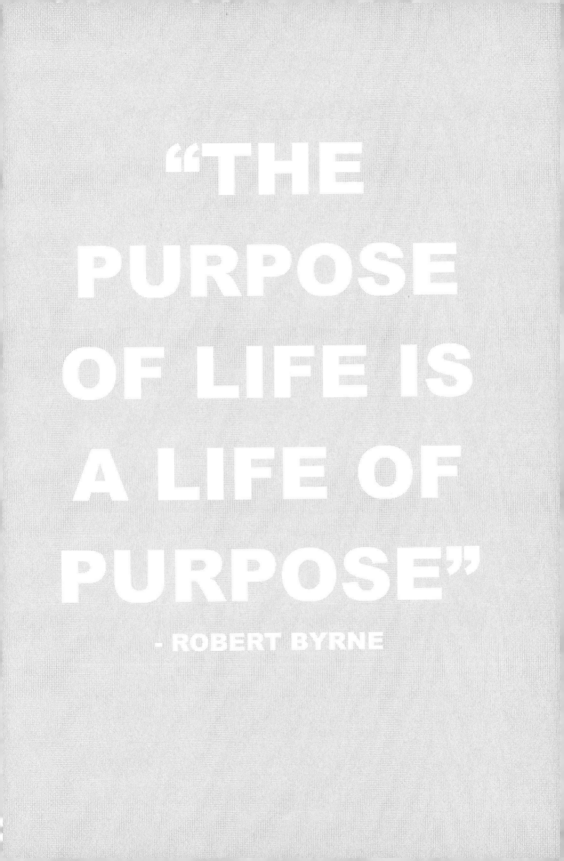

"THE PURPOSE OF LIFE IS A LIFE OF PURPOSE"

- ROBERT BYRNE

DASHBOARDS

PERSONAL SUCCESS STATEMENTS

Directions: Fill in the frequency, action verb, and measurement for the three personal success statements below.

Example: By the end <u>*of my life*</u>, I want to have <u>*inspired a*</u>
                          Frequency   Action Verb
<u>*10,000,000 people to live more purpose-filled lives*</u>
Quantity   Area of Measurement

Quote: "The purpose of life is a life of purpose." — Robert Byrne

1. By the end ...., I want to have ....
                Frequency   Action Verb   Quantity

....
                      Area of Measurement

2. By the end ...., I want to have ....
                Frequency   Action Verb   Quantity

....
                      Area of Measurement

3. By the end ...., I want to have ....
                Frequency   Action Verb   Quantity

....
                      Area of Measurement

DASHBOARDS

PROFESSIONAL SUCCESS STATEMENTS

Directions: Fill in the frequency, action verb, and measurement for the three professional success statements below.

Example: By the end <u>*my career*</u>, I want to have <u>*created*</u>
                              Frequency   Action Verb
<u>*products that make*</u> *a 1,000,000 customers say wow!*
                          Quantity   Area of Measurement

Quote: "The real bottom line is customer service."

1. By the end ...., I want to have ....
                    Frequency   Action Verb   Quantity

....
                         Area of Measurement

2. By the end ...., I want to have ....
                    Frequency   Action Verb   Quantity

....
                         Area of Measurement

3. By the end ...., I want to have ....
                    Frequency   Action Verb   Quantity

....
                         Area of Measurement

MOVE-MEANT

Where The Rubber Meets The Road

Below are specific actions you can do in the next 30 days to align your life a little bit more with your personal and professional principles.

Personal: Share your personal dashboard with your family and friends so that they are aware of how you measure success and ask them to support you on your journey.

Professional: Visualize your professional dashboard to the best of your ability using bar graphs, pie charts, and other images and then share it with your manager and/or team to make sure that you are aligned with their expectations of you. Also ask for new strategies and projects that will allow you score higher on your dashboard.

MONEY,
FAME,
& BEAUTY
ARE NOT
THE ONLY WAYS
TO MEASURE
SUCCESS

PASSIONS » YOUR KEYS

THE PURPOSE OF THIS CHAPTER IS TO:

- Translate part-time passions into your full-time profession
- Differentiate passions from interests
- Evaluate how much time per week you spend using your passions

GUIDING QUEST-IONS:

Personal: What do I love doing and why?

Professional: What are my company's competitive advantages and strengths? What strengths am I exercising and developing while at my company?

QUOTES:

A strong passion for any object will ensure success, for the desire of the end will point out the means."
— William Hazlitt

"A great leader's courage to fulfill his vision comes from passion, not position."
— John Maxwell

STEVE IRWIN'S PASSIONS: WILDLIFE & CONSERVATION

At the age of nine, I was *passively* watching the likes of the Hulk Hogan and the Ultimate Warrior wrestle. Steve Irwin a.k.a. The Crocodile Hunter was *actively* wrestling with crocodiles when he was nine. Born to parents who shared a passion for wildlife, Irwin basically grew up in a zoo. At age six, Irwin received a four-meter python as a birthday gift and our first memorable toy can say a lot about our passions. Whereas most parents lovingly push their children to secure paths, Irwin's parents nurtured his risk-taking and desire for adventure. When he was a child, they started the small Queensland Reptile and Fauna Park in Australia, which he later took over at the age of 30 and grew into the Australia Zoo. Four years later, *The Crocodile Hunter* television series aired for the first time in Australia, and in less than five years, he reached over 500 million people in 137 countries with his message about wildlife and conservation.

Irwin was driven by more than off-road vehicles. He was motivated by a desire to end poaching, land clearing, and kangaroo culling. He said, "I consider myself a wildlife warrior. My mission is to save the world's endangered species." Though he was exercising his passions for wildlife, he was also changing global perceptions about human beings' relationship with animals and nature through his work. He was off-road in thought and action. Before Irwin, most people only experienced nature through magazine pages and zoo gates, but he brought nature into people's homes through his show and passionate personality. Being the pioneer he was, he revolutionized viewer's relationship with nature saying:

"We've evolved from sitting back on our tripods and shooting wildlife films like they have been shot historically, which doesn't work for us. When I talk to the camera, mate, it's not like I'm talking to the camera, I'm talking to you because I want to whip you around and plunk you right there with me."

Irwin's influence has led to present day shows like Bear Grylls' *Man vs. Wild* and Les Stround's *Survivor Man.*

Whether you watched *The Crocodile Hunter* openly, secretly, or not at all, we all have a to desire to be as passionate about something as deeply as Irwin was about wildlife and conservation. Unfortunately, at age 44, Irwin was killed when he was struck in the chest with a stingray's barb while filming on the Great Barrier Reef in 2006. Fear of failure often stops people from doing what they love. **Since he did what he loved every day, he was guaranteed to die doing what he loved.** Even though Irwin didn't project fear through the television screen, he even he says, "I suffer from fear like everyone else." We only fear death when we haven't lived. **The opposite of fear of failure is certainty of success, but certainty cheats us of the adventure of life.** Imagine being destined for success and knowing exactly how that success would come about. It would be boring if life was predictable.

MY PASSIONS: BUILDING COMMUNITY & CREATING TRANSFORMATION COLLECTIVE EXPERIENCES

From the time I was introduced to the concept of leadership during my junior year of high school, my passion has been motivating people through building community and creating collective experiences. My parents, sports coaches, professors, and faculty always saw potential in me and encouraged me to challenge myself through leadership. Toward the end of my junior year in high school, three new leadership opportunities came my way all at once, which made for a phenomenal senior year: vice president of my high school, head coach of my little brother's soccer team, and a member of the select campus ministry team.

We often have to look back into the past to discover our passions, especially the times before the "real" world set in. However, instead of just looking at the positions we took on, we need to explore our projects and actions in those positions to discover our passions. As vice president of the school I, along with the rest of the executive team, was responsible for screening the talent show acts for the campus-wide Spirit Week. I explicitly remember four hip-hop acts from each class trying out for the show. Collectively, the executive team chose not to select any of them for the show. However, I came up with an idea to create a unity act among all four classes where they performed together. Not only was their performance the highlight on the evening, but it also embodied the purpose of Spirit Week.

As a soccer coach, I came to learn that soccer was just a vehicle to teach young men about themselves and life in the same way sports and my coaches taught me. Finally, as a member of the Campus Ministry Team, we were responsible for building campus-wide community through retreats, liturgies, and other programming. In hindsight, these experiences allowed me to exercise a passion that I didn't have words to describe at the time.

Since then, my passion for motivating people through building community and creating collective experiences has manifested itself in many ways. I can only see the patterns and reoccurring themes in the various spaces I've been a part of in hindsight or by looking through my life's rear view mirror.

While at UCLA I:

- Created a financial literacy organization called STOCKS & BONDS
- Reignited the African Men's Collective which also produced the Black Love Forum and Beautiful Struggle Conference
- Led Think Tanks every Wednesday at my home for personal empowerment
- Co-chaired the largest high school conference for urban youth
- Created and facilitated curriculum for foster youth preparing for emancipation

While running the S.H.A.P.E. program I:

- Create curriculum for peer advising and skill building
- Facilitated retreats for student leaders on campus

- Created and facilitated curriculum for high school students preparing for work

While at Stanford I:

- Co-facilitated the BBSA annual retreat
- Created the Hall of Understanding as part of the campus diversity team
- United our graduating class as part of the Capstone Event planning committee
- Started hosting weekly potlucks with a group of friends to feed people spiritually, mentally, and physically

And now, as the Founder and CEO of the Department of Motivated Vehicles, I am doing the same work through my Driving School for Life course and community. What you see above is not a resume; it's an inventory of my passions. Despite the variety of positions I had as a student, program director, and CEO, there are striking similarities between how I used each position to exercise my passions.

As you take an inventory of your passions, consider what type of projects or activities you gravitated towards and then use that to identify new positions or professions that will allow you to do your passions in the future. To expand your inventory beyond work and extracurricular activities, you can also look at a variety of things including: your favorite subject in school, subject outside of school, topics to debate about, TV shows, musicians, sports, books, movies, websites, games, super heroes, placed to hand, things to do alone, and things to do with others. After considering your list of favorite, consider what passions are connected to each activity and see if you discover any patterns. See the Passion Finder exercise at the end of the chapter.

PASSIONS AS KEYS

Your passions are the keys that get your vehicle started. On the journey of life, passions are the activities that ignite you and get you fired up when you do them, hear about them, see them, or talk about them. Only you hold the key to your passions. However, your key chain may have many keys to choose from or very few. Sometimes we have keys on our key chain that we don't even use anymore. It is important to let them go to free up space in your home and your life for the ones you use regularly or new ones. The ultimate goal is to find the set of keys that set your vehicle into motion.

Every year you start your cars at least 1,000 times. Like your keys, your passions unlock vital doors and you should use them every day. If you simply ignited your passion as often as you start up your car, you would get more mileage out of life. All drivers think they drive well because they drive every day. But when it comes to your passions, you don't treat them the same, despite knowing that daily dedication helped many of the people we call greats achieve their greatness. When we look at a lot of celebrities today like Tiger Woods, Bobby Fischer, and Michael Jackson we know that golf, chess, and singing were part of their lives since childhood. Though they have been using the same key to start the same car over and over and over again, their vehicles to success gained value over time because of regular tuning and use. **Most vehicles die for two reasons: too much use combined**

with too little maintenance or no use at all. Most people's passions die because of low usage.

Have you ever lost your keys? The first thing you do is panic. You know that without your keys, you are stuck— you can't go anywhere because you need your keys to get started. **Since your keys are part of your daily routine, they should have their own place in your life, like on the mantle or dresser.** Even so, sometimes you lose your keys like you lose your passions.

Like our keys, the best way to recover your passions is to retrace your steps by asking yourself, "Where was I when I last had them?" This process usually requires going back to your childhood. Much like the way you recover your keys, you can recover your passion for life with a few simple steps. As children, if we were exposed to a wide variety of options, we naturally gravitated towards the things that we loved doing and we can find evidence in our photo albums, family stories, bookshelves, music collection, or parents' garages. If you were not exposed to many things as a child, then you likely had to choose what interested you most based on what was available, which cuts off a lot of possibilities. Passions begin as interests and one interest can lead to another, which leads to another until you finally find an interest that you're committed to making a passion.

Malcolm Gladwell's book *Outlier* dispels common myths we have about success, such as people being born better than others. He also discusses the notion of 10,000 hours or 10 years (20 hrs/week 50 weeks for 10 years = 10,000 hours) of practice being the prerequisite for success. He recounts Bill Gates' story beginning in high school where he was given access to a rare state-of-the-art computer that allowed him to practice, practice, and practice his passion to a point where he crystallized his passion for technology into a valuable skill. By the time other technological innovations occurred, he was positioned to capitalize on the opportunities and create Microsoft. **Bill Gates demonstrated that once passions transform into skills, they become valuable to the marketplace and the sticker price on your vehicle shoots up.** Otherwise, our passions remain confined to hobbies.

Talented people aren't entitled to anything they don't earn through focused effort. Any sense of **en-title-meant (feeling deserving of a title without putting in the required effort to earn it)** distorts one's perception of what is actually theirs like a teenager who thinks his parent's old car is his because he believes he is *supposed* to get a car in high school like his friends. **Those who believe in natural talent believe that everyone has a natural talent except them.** But when you ask talented people about their talents, they share how they discovered them *and* most importantly how they developed them over time. **Most people never discover a talent to develop because of limited exposure and experience. The more avenues of interests we are exposed to, especially as children, the more likely we are to find an intersection where something we are passionate about crosses with something we're great at doing.** We are born with many interests, but interests are just the seeds of passions. In order for any seed to grow it needs time and energy.

The energy derived from practicing our passions is infinite because it is sourced from within. It's when we fail to start our cars for a long period of time that the battery eventually dies and needs to be replaced or recharged. **In fact, the more you use your passions, the more passionate you become. That's why it's your edge.** In business, a competitive advantage is defined as a positional power that one firm has against another due to their unique competencies, capabilities, or access to resources. **Likewise, a passionate person will always outlast a non-passionate person in any endeavor because they get more mileage per gallon—they have an unfair advantage.** It's a lot less costly on your mind, body, and soul to live in a-line-meant with your passions because they usually come easier to you than anything else. **Passionate people re-energize on their own like hybrid cars.** They don't rely on outside things—like materials, money, coffee, and drugs—to motivate them. They are self-motivated.

By making the same commitment to your passions as you do to your car, they will take you places that cars can't go. If your passion is photography, then shoot at least one photo every day. If your passion is interacting with customers, then shift as much of your work schedule as possible to doing that. The only way to crystallize a passion into a valuable skill is to use it so often that people around you begin to recognize you and rely on you for it. People who are the best at something in their company or community typically create and capture the most value in terms of money and opportunities long-term. **Aligning your passion and profession is the ultimate form of job security because it makes you hard to replace.**

You can tell how passionate someone is by how they relate to that passion. When they hear anyone even mention a word from that domain, they start eavesdropping on the conversation. When someone is doing something they love, they are in their own world and glow as they move almost effortlessly through the activity. When someone is talking about his or her passions, they use jargon relevant to their lane or field, mention historical events, cite names, and quote people you have never heard of. When someone is developing their passion, they are focused and learning as if they were studying for an exam. When you're doing your passion, you emit a radiant energy that is unmistakable.

Passionate people also begin to look at life through the lens of their passions and make analogies about life using their passion. Through the mastery of your passions, you can actually achieve self-mastery. One of the best metaphors about life I heard came from an avid bike rider who said, "Life is like riding a fixed gear bike, you get what you put in." A fixed gear bike moves at the rate you pedal. To stop the bike, you stop pedaling and it skids. It takes a passionate person to understand their passion so deeply that they can extract life lessons from the actual practice of the passion.

We're usually using our passion in some way already, but we're not conscious of it enough to be deliberate about it. Talking to another friend who is *deeply* passionate about archeology (pun intended) and is currently in a recruiting role for a Fortune 500 company, I challenged her to look at her current job as "digging" for the fossilized talent within prospective employees. It was an "ah-ha" moment for her and changed the way she thought about her current job. An archeologist is someone who spends their time *digging* for information, *connecting* historical events, and *studying*

people. As a recruiter, she spends her time *digging* through resumes, *connecting* academic and career paths, and *studying* prospective candidates. Without being fully aware, her passion for archaeology manifested as a professional recruiter.

PASSIONS VS. INTERESTS

Passions often get confused with interests. Interests are the seeds of passions, but they only become passions once they mature and the person commits time to deepening their relationship with the passion. Our passions have to do with how we spend our time and how we engage with the world, therefore, they should be written and communicated in the action verb form ending with "-ing." Whereas *baseball* is just an interest, *playing baseball* is a passion. The action defines the relationship between the person, passion, and interest.

PASSIONS VS. INTERESTS

PASSIONS	INTERESTS
Action-oriented (playing baseball, coaching baseball)	General and Topical (i.e. baseball)
Long-term	Short-term
Inspire and enthuse indefinitely	Motivate & excite momentarily
Matured interest	The seed of passion
Full-time (make time for it)	Free-time (if there is time for it)
Self-initiated	Initiated by others
Disciplined practice	Half-hearted play
Dedication	Dabbling

Interest + Action = Passion. When there is an action associated with the interest, it becomes clear on how to practice that passion. When it comes to physical passions, defining how to exercise that passion is evident. In order to become a better hitter, you hit. In order to become a better catcher, you catch. In order to become a better pitcher, you pitch. And together, those skills make up a great baseball player. When you practice your passions, they crystallize into skills or ways to create value, while part-time interests just become hobbies. We each have to define the game that we are playing and figure out what skills will make us the M.V.P. (most valuable player) we can be in that game.

INTERESTS & ASSOCIATED PASSIONS

INTERESTS	ASSOCIATED PASSIONS
Baseball	throwing baseball, coaching baseball, collecting baseball cards, hitting baseballs, watching baseball
Health	healing, nursing, medicating, restoring, counseling
Cooking	hosting, serving, growing food, creating menus

THE SOURCE OF OUR PASSIONS

Over the course of our lives, we experiment with many interests. I remember being a ten-year-old soccer player with dreams of becoming the next Cobi Jones, a top U.S. soccer player at the time. My passion for soccer was at its peak, but as I got older, my passion faded. Three things typically happen with our passions:

1. They either fade because we are told that we can't make a living doing our passion so we *ignore* instead of *ignite* them
2. Our passions get overlooked because they come so naturally to us and we don't know how great we really are at them, or
3. Our passion shifts to something else to frequently to become great

During my junior year in high school, basketball became the cool thing to do, so I shifted my time and energy to practicing basketball instead of soccer even though I was a better midfielder than point guard. Though I got pretty good at basketball, my true passion was soccer. I coached my little brother's under-12 team for two years during high school, but I didn't pick up soccer again as a player until my senior year of high school after getting cut from the varsity basketball team.

Sometimes our passions come so naturally to us that we simply overlook them. We assume that because they have always come so easily to us that they probably come easily to others as well, and therefore we write them off. Our passions are all around us and they reveal themselves when we are just being ourselves. Anytime a friend says, "How did you do that?" or, "You're really good at that," you should receive these as clues to dis-covering your unique passions.

Friends: Email or text your friends and simply ask them, "What would you say I'm most passionate about?" You will receive answers that resonate with you and ones that throw you off. Every answer you receive is information about yourself that you've projected. If there is consistency among the answers it means that you're doing an amazing job of conveying your passions wherever you are, to everyone around you. If there is inconsistency or if you get general answers like, "You're good with people" or, "You're passionate about life," then you haven't effectively communicated through your thoughts, words, and actions what you are truly passionate about to your friends and colleagues.

Free Work: Free work is another way to discover one's passions because the person has the freedom to choose where they want to spend their time and mind without money or fear of failure being issues. Don't mistake free work for volunteering. **Volunteering means doing something like cleaning up the beach because it's inherently a good thing to do despite the fact that you know it isn't where you add the most value to the world. Free work means identifying your passions and sharing it with the world in whatever way you can for free.** When we are serving in this way, there are no start-up costs and fear of failure is absent.

Passionate people are also willing to endure failure at their passion whereas a less passionate person won't. A person who is passionate about something will find a way to do it with or without money. Even with almost half a billion dollars in the bank, you couldn't pay Jay-Z to stop rapping. He's come out of retirement three times now. The same goes for Michael Jordan who retired from professional basketball three times. **We don't retire from our passions—we simply re-tire, and change roles by changing roads.**

Bedroom: Your inner passion should be reflected in your outer world. Clues about your passion can be found in your bedroom, your cell phone, your wallet, your calendar, your bookshelf, your internet bookmarks, and your email account. Your passions shape the art in your home, your friends, your membership cards, the events you go to, the books you read, the websites you browse, the newsletters and magazines you subscribe to, and the things you buy. You're likely carrying something with you right now that expresses your passion, like a camera, pen, iPod, skateboard, or bike helmet. **Your passions consume you and you consume them.**

PERSONAL KEYS

Ultimately, you want to align your passions with your strengths. Passions don't develop naturally, but you naturally gravitate toward them when you are seriously searching for them by trying out new interests. Greatness works similarly. It has been said that, "Repetition is the father of learning." Greatness only comes through repetition and self-discipline. **Self-discipline has a negative connotation when you're doing something you don't want to do, but the passionate person sees self-discipline in a positive light because they want to be doing that activity.** That which is difficult to others almost comes effortlessly to those who are passionate about the task at hand.

This effortlessness is captured in the word "flow," used by positive psychologist, Mihaly Csikszentmihalyi, to describe what athletes call "in the zone." It is the mental state of operation in which the person is fully immersed in what he or she is doing by a feeling of energized focus, full involvement, and success in the process of the activity. In his book, *Finding Flow*, Csikszentmihalyi states that, "Flow is generally reported when a person is doing his or her favorite activity—gardening, listening to music, bowling, cooking a good meal." According to him, happiness isn't enough by itself, happiness comes from *how you do what you do*. Therefore, your passions offer you an opportunity to love what you do in the same way you would love another human being so that you stay engaged and in flow.

In the book, *Success Built to Last*, Jerry Porras, Stewart Emery, and Mark Thompson, interviewed hundreds of "successful" people—including many Nobel Laureates, government and community service leaders, teachers, scientists, and Olympians, as well as Pulitzer, Grammy, Peabody, and Academy Award winners—to identify common characteristics among them. Success was defined as having at least two decades of impact in one's industry, field, or lane.

They discovered that successful people don't obsess over what other people may think about their work. They also found that enduringly successful people are more concerned with doing what they love than being loved. They don't treat their passions like a trivial pursuits or low-priority items. Successful people focus on being good at what is meaningful to them, and do that—not "whatever" just comes along. They understand their unique passions and allocate their view of the right amount of time to each, according to their own individually chosen preference.

Our careers are simply avenues for us to exercise our purpose and passions. The etymology of the word career evolves from the medieval Latin word carraria meaning road for vehicles. **Looked at another way, the word career can be seen as *care*-er, which suggests that our career should be something that we *care* about and has meaning to us.** If we want to create value we have to do that which we value and your career serves as the best space for us to express your value.

PROFESSIONAL KEYS

Imagine that the job you're currently in is simply practice for the job you really want. When you're ready to interview for your dream job, what skills will you be able to say you developed through your current job? The practice of your passions develops skills that can be applied to your profession. It is important to define the action so that you can consciously practice the passion daily. Most professional athletes practice more than they actually play, but the balance of practice and play depends on your unique passions. Playing can be a part of your practice plan to test your skills, but it cannot encompass the entire plan.

Both my parents are doctors and doctors practice medicine. I've never heard anyone say "I'm doctoring right now." Whereas doctors say they *practice*, as children we used to *play* doctor. We weren't practicing it to get better; we simply played it to have fun. In the same way, to become a better entrepreneur you don't entrepreneur. You can be interested in entrepreneurship in general, but related passions would be starting companies, managing people, solving problems, and creating value. Entrepreneurs start their businesses for a variety of reasons beyond their desire to be an entrepreneur.

Passions rarely get acknowledged as skills. When people think of passions, they tend to only think about hobbies like playing sports, painting, traveling, and cooking. But passions transcend physical activity and weekends. Passions can also be professional or mental skills such as communicating with people, developing strategy, managing processes, marketing, and budgeting. There are people who love doing these things as much as a child loves playing outside.

Unfortunately, the world is plagued by underemployment and human resource misallocation. **There are doctors who really want to be artists. Artists who want to be teachers. And teachers who want to be doctors.** For whatever reason, people choose professional paths that aren't in a-line-meant with their passions, who they want to be, and what they want to do. Meanwhile someone who doesn't love it as much as they do is making a living doing it.

Many people take jobs just because they are available but being underemployed is worse than being unemployed and searching. When you are unaware of your own self-worth you are open to offers to do things you don't like because an offer suggests that someone values you. Before moving too quickly, you should examine why the position is open in the first place, especially if it's not a new position. **The worst thing a young professional can do is take the first job that comes to them without assessing its a-line-meant with their personal and professional goals.**

Before inter-viewing for a new position, we must first inner-view. Inter-viewing is the exchange of

COMPANY PROFILE:
PASSIONS & PATAGONIA

One modern-day story of a passionate entrepreneur and company is that of Yvon Chouinard, founder Patagonia, a man who is saving the world one fleece jacket at a time. Chouinard is a legendary climber, surfer, entrepreneur, environmentalist, and philanthropist. He started the company in the 1950s and over time combined his passions for climbing, clothing, and climate change all together to create one of the most environmentally-friendly clothing companies in the world.

Below is Patagonia's mission statement and history as described on their corporate website.

Mission Statement:

"Build the best product, cause no unnecessary harm, use business to inspire and implement solutions to the environmental crisis."

Company History:

"Patagonia grew out of a small company that made tools for climbers. Alpinism remains at the heart of a worldwide business that still makes clothes for climbing – as well as for skiing, snowboarding, surfing, fly fishing, paddling and trail running. These are all silent sports. None requires a motor; none delivers the cheers of a crowd. In each sport, reward comes in the form of hard-won grace and moments of connection between us and nature.

Our values reflect those of a business started by a band of climbers and surfers, and the minimalist style they promoted. The approach we take towards product design demonstrates a bias for simplicity and utility.

For us at Patagonia, a love of wild and beautiful places demands participation in the fight to save them, and to help reverse the steep decline in the overall environmental health of our planet. We donate our time, services and at least 1% of our sales to hundreds of grassroots environmental groups all over the world who work to help reverse the tide.

We know that our business activity – from lighting stores to dyeing shirts – creates pollution as a by-product. So we work steadily to reduce those harms. We use recycled polyester in many of our clothes and only organic, rather than pesticide-intensive, cotton.

Staying true to our core values during thirty-plus years in business has helped us create a company we're proud to run and work for. And our focus on making the best products possible has brought us success in the marketplace."

Patagonia has successfully weaved their passion into every aspect of their business and as a result is able to attract talented employees who share its passion for the environment.

information between an individual and a company to see if there is interest. Inner-viewing is the process of assessing one's passions, strengths, and fit for a position prior to any inter-view. We often skip the inner-viewing process just to get a job, when in fact, the inner-viewing process will increase your chances of getting the job you want with fewer inter-views. Most people focus all of their energy on the inter-viewing process and get lazy on the inner-view and search processes. By taking time to refine your search, you can achieve better search results, and thus limit the amount of inter-views and rejections.

Let's say you take an undesirable job because you need the money and have student loans to pay. **Where you spend your time is where you get refined and the second worst thing that any young professional can do to themselves is get great at what they hate.** Just because someone is great at something doesn't mean that they love it or that it is what they were put here to do. We can become great at almost anything in the world with enough practice. The challenge is that when someone gets great at something, they end up attracting more of it, even if they don't like doing it that much and it isn't in a-line-meant with their purpose. **In Hollywood, this is called type-casting. Someone takes on a role that they don't necessarily like, they succeed at it, and then after that, all they get is offers to do similar roles. It's a dangerous path to test.**

If you find yourself in this situation, I highly recommend taking a bridge job. **A bridge job is a short-term job that will allow you to develop intellectual, social, or financial capital to position yourself for the job you really want.** The bridge should be no longer than 18 months if you're taking it for intellectual and social reasons. If you're taking it for financial reasons, the goal should be to save up to cover four months of expenses (= 4 x your minimum monthly expenses). Knowing that the job is a bridge job will force you to extract as much value from the experience as you can and it will force you to keep your living expenses down. **Too many people trap themselves by raising their living expenses with car payments, mortgages or higher rent. These perceived luxuries actually restrict financial freedom at this stage of life and should be delayed as long as possible so that you have the flexibility to find a profession that matches your true passion first.**

MANY PASSIONS

Before industrialization and globalization, people lived in small communities and each person in that community had a particular role. There was the grocer, blacksmith, doctor, teacher, preacher, farmer, and hunter. It was clear what your role in the community was and that was the only thing you did. Many companies still operate like this today, though some are learning to view their employees as a talent pool of passions to be used according to the company strategy at the given moment, rather than expendable parts that only serve a singular function. Nowadays, people have multiple passions and find it extremely difficult to integrate them without compromising one or the other. Ironically, some of the world's greatest innovators and most successful people have been those who have found creative ways to combine two or more passions that previously appeared unrelated.

Sometimes the more distant one's various passions seem, the more innovative the ideas are that come from the person. According to Wikipedia, emergence is a scientific theory that explains the way complex systems and patterns arise out of a multiplicity of relatively simple interactions. The same theory supports organizational behavior claims that diverse and cross-functional teams produce more innovative ideas than homogeneous teams. Having multiple passions is a strength as long as you can find time to stay ahead in both. The moment it starts to feel like dabbling, you should stop, identify which ones are interests and which ones are passions using the Passions vs. Interests chart from earlier, and then refocus on mastering one or two of your passions.

PASSIONS AS SKILLS

There are creative ways to make your part-time passions transferable skills for your full-time jobs if you think beyond the traditional uses. For example, a person who is passionate about chess understands strategy, forward-thinking, and risk-taking. If they simply look at their business environment as a big chess board, then they can apply their strategic thinking skills from their part-time passion to their full-time profession. A person passionate about bargain shopping can see the business world as one huge garage sale and translate their weekend shopping skills into weekday mergers and acquisitions. Once you've identified your passions, you need to think creatively about how they help you grow and how they apply to the world around you beyond the actual action itself. Sometimes there isn't a direct correlation between your passion and a profession, so you must begin with the question "What is it about this activity that I love?" Thinking about the part of the activity (i.e. forward-thinking) and the feelings it evokes may give you insight into what part of the activity moves you most and then you can look for that particular aspect in other opportunities.

You can begin this process by breaking down your interests into related actions and related emotions. Let's use cooking as an example. The cooking process involves a series of actions: creating the menu, grocery shopping, preparing the food, cooking the food, serving the meal, cleaning the dishes, and putting away the dishes. It is rare to find someone who is passionate about every part of the cooking process—not even chefs. If a chef only likes preparing, cooking, and serving, they need to find another foodie who loves creating the menu and shopping for food as much as the chef loves their parts of the process. It also involves the emotions of giving, punctuality, creativity, gratitude, and praise. **The goal is to get all of the stuff off of your plate that you don't like onto the plate of someone who loves it. This is how great teams are built.**

Another way to examine your part-time passion is through the feelings it evokes. A lot of our decisions are driven by the perceived feeling we're going to receive from the action or outcome. When we were younger, we said we wanted to pursue career paths like doctors because of the feelings we thought it would bring us. That lasted until some of us saw blood by the gallon for the first time and got a noxious contrary feeling that steered us toward an alternate professional path like law or business. Feelings can come from the process or the result. For instance an archaeologist may value the feelings of exhilaration, excitement, and adventure from the exploration process and they may value the feelings of praise, excellence, and celebrity that come from making a ground-breaking discovery.

This view of passions may change how you perceive career opportunities inside and outside of your current company and how you position yourself to capitalize on them. It may also change what majors, minors, and activities HR departments look for when they hire. A lot of people hope to find their passion in their careers. Instead, you should start with finding your passions and then choose a career, not vice versa.

MONETIZING PASSIONS

People are getting paid to practice the most obscure passions as their profession. When things are obscure, they are rare. According to the law of supply and demand, careers with short supplies of potential employees are able to command great salaries. But in order to land a career like that you have to be the best at what you do. **Most people just wade in their passions by sticking their big toe in the kiddy pool, but greatness requires full immersion if you want to get paid to do what you love.** And in order to be great, we have to define what practice is for our passion.

Practicing physical passions is pretty straightforward, while practicing mental passions is a lot more difficult. Though practice is unpaid, it is the key ingredient to becoming a professional in any industry where you can potentially get paid for your passion. It's assumed that education is practice for your career, but in most cases it's not. Therefore, by practicing or interning on top of your education, you can set yourself apart from everyone else.

Most people believe that economic success leads to their passions, therefore they seek a job to make money to buy time to do what they love. That's backwards. We should use the time we have to discover and do what we love and find or create a job that will pay us to do it. For every passion in the world, I can probably name a person, job, or company where someone is making a living doing your passion daily. Beginning with your passions leads to economic success.

The myth of the starving artist is perhaps the number one killer of passion. The underlying message of the starving artist is that you can't make a living doing what you love. In a way, we're all artists because we're all creators, whether we're creating art, businesses, strategies, or new solutions for an existing company. Whatever you spend most of your thought energy on will become your craft. Whatever you're currently doing, make sure that a technological solution can't replace you in five to ten years. Anything that can be automated will be and you will have spent your entire career developing a skill set that is worthless.

Most adults work full-time at something, but the question is whether or not people are employing their passions full-time. By this definition of employment, most people are *underemployed* which also means that they are probably not productive, not positive, and not profitable. Passions should and can be full-time, not just part-time. You don't have to compromise your passions for your profession. The challenge is converting your passions into crystallized skills.

The ability to crystallize your passions into tangible skills is what separates the 10-year-old dreamer who becomes a full-time day-dreamer from the passionate professional who has made their dream a reality. According to William Damon, author of *The Path To Purpose*, there are four types of young people based on the sense of purpose they express in their lives: the nonpurposeful, the dreamer, the dabbler, and the purposeful. The nonpurposeful and the dreamers each make up 25% of the national sample, while the dabblers accounted for 31% and the purposeful made up the final 20%. Damon defines dreamers as "those who express ideas about purposes that they would like to have, but who have done little or nothing actively to try out any of their ideas." Essentially, dreamers are drivers without keys, and their vehicle is stuck until they find them.

If you don't feel like you're living a life full of passion right now, then the best way to search for your passion is to analyze how you spend your mental time. If there is a difference between where you spend your *mind* and where you spend your *time*, it is hard to be fully present in anything that you are doing and therefore you cannot compete with the person who is fully present. **The key is to align your *mind* and your *time* so that you are fully engaged in what you are doing. Too many people *marry* themselves to companies without ever getting *engaged*. This is the precursor to professional (and occasionally family) divorce.**

CONCLUSION

Over time a few of my passions have crystallized into skills: organizing information, creating collective experiences, uniting diverse groups, collaging (the process of pulling ideas, images, and words together to make a cohesive idea), making metaphors, coaching, public-speaking and presenting ideas. Some of them are self-serving and some serve others. Some are mental and others are physical. Despite the variations, they are all important to my happiness and my unique purpose.

We all have things that we love to do, even if you're can't articulate them. I don't know of anyone who is truly happy doing nothing. **You need breaks, escapes, and vacations from the things you don't like, but your passions are where you vacate to because they allow you to be fully expressed in the world.** Whether your passions just add value to you (i.e. collecting stamps, swimming, reading) or they add value for you and others (i.e. serving, consulting, teaching, etc.), by simply sharing why you do what you do with others may expose them to a new way of thinking about their passions and help them discover a new way of facilitating their own happiness. Ask yourself, "Am I striving to make that which makes me happiest available to anyone who wants to participate?" **Regardless of which type of passions you have, passions serve as our personal platform for growth and help us achieve self-mastery as we seek to master them.**

PASSION FINDER

Directions: Complete the chart below with your favorite things to do and their associated passions. Finally, weave together the various passion to create a one sentence passion statement that is unique to you.

Favorites My favorite...	Passions This speaks to my passion for....
The Alchemist	*Seeking truth, finding self*
THING TO DO ALONE	
THING TO DO WITH OTHERS	
THING TO DO AT WORK	
SUBJECT IN SCHOOL	
SUBJECT OUT OF SCHOOL	
TELEVISION SHOW	
BOOK	
MOVIE	
WEBSITE	
SUPERHERO/ CHARACTER	
ORGANIZATION	

My passion is...

....

MOVE-MEANT

Where The Rubber Meets The Road

Below are specific actions you can do in the next 30 days to align your life a little bit more with your personal and professional passions.

Personal: Set aside one hour a day in the morning, during lunch, or after work to practice your passions more. Schedule it into your week just like you would schedule an appointment or meeting. You may consider taking a class, joining a group, or looking for related events.

Professional: Share your passions with your manager or colleagues. Express that you feel you could create more value if you got assignments that allowed you to use your passions. Seek to reallocate your time by negotiating to get something off of your plate that you're not passionate about doing and replace it with more of something you are truly passionate about doing.

PROBLEMS »
YOUR FUEL

THE PURPOSE OF THIS CHAPTER IS TO:

- Identify the problem or cause that moves you most
- Create a guiding question for your quest

GUIDING QUEST-IONS:

Personal: What social, scientific, technical, or personal problem do I want to solve?

Professional: What is my company's customers' personal, social, scientific, or technical problem? What related problems do I get to solve?

QUOTES:

"The significant problems we face cannot be solved at the same level of thinking we were at when we created them."
— Albert Einstein

"Irritation, not necessity, is the true "mother of invention."
— Unknown

MUHAMMAD YUNUS' PROBLEM: POVERTY & ACCESS TO CAPITAL

During the 1974 Bangladeshi famine, Muhammad Yunus visited the country for a research project. During his visit he met a group of 42 families who were struggling to make ends meet. He was moved to make a small loan of $27 to them so that they could create small items for sale without the burdens of extremely high interest rates from local financiers. His experience revealed that the poor are bankable and have higher repayment rates than people who are loaned money and have higher incomes. His initial loan led to the creation of the Grameen Bank in 1983. After 25 years of scaling this local solution, the Grameen Bank has an operating income of over $90M.

The root cause of poverty has always been access to capital. But there were general assumptions that poor people were not reliable, not hard working, and not smart, until economist Yunus experienced the opposite. He combined his passion for economics with the problem of poverty. Though the connection seems obvious, despite millions of economists before him, Yunus was the first to create the concept of microfinance, which refers to the provision of financial services to poor or low-income clients, including consumers and the self-employed. Yunus saw the poor as merely undercapitalized entrepreneurs who deserved fair loan agreements so that their businesses and families could flourish.

Yunus' work has led people to call him the Banker to the Poor. Bankers don't donate, they make smart loans. Fighting poverty through donations and charity feel good to do, but they aren't true **soul-utions (solutions that affect people from the inside out versus the outside in)**—the root of the problem still exists no matter how much money is raised. Access to capital is the key. Hopefully one day we will transcend microfinance and all entrepreneurial people with great ideas and business models will be financed fairly (with no 'micro' before the word finance). Only then will we embark on a road to the end of poverty.

MY PROBLEMS: UNDEREMPLOYMENT & ITS SIDE EFFECTS

My search for purpose began in 5th grade when my mother became an alcoholic. Actually, she became a victim of purposelessness—alcoholism just happened to be the way it manifested itself. It is important to differentiate between the source of a problem and the symptoms. Alcohol was not the problem, purposelessness was. All her life, she wanted to be a photographer, but was discouraged from doing so because of the myth of the starving artists. Every time I heard this, I couldn't help but look up at a photo or painting on a nearby wall which let me know that it was possible to eat off art. As a child, I remember hating to take pictures because while most parents only brought a camera to recitals and graduations, my mom had a camera for everything. Little did I know that by avoiding her pictures, I was robbing her of her passion.

She was born during a generation when the underlying belief was that if you got a professional degree (i.e. doctor, lawyer), you were guaranteed happiness, so she was encouraged to pursue medicine and became an anesthesiologist because she lacked the courage within and community around her to do what she really wanted to. At the time, it was rare for a Black woman to pursue this profession, therefore, it was a great accomplishment and a source of pride. But even her pride couldn't fill her sense of emptiness. Despite making six-figures, owning a huge three-story house in one of Oakland's best neighborhoods, and driving a Mercedes Benz, the belief that higher education guaranteed happiness proved false. **My mother's experience has taught me that the only education that guarantees happiness is self-education—knowing who you are and why you are here.**

As her profession went one way, her passion went the other way. A canyon was created in her life and she filled that depression with alcohol. Years of medical school and over a decade of professional practice killed her creative spirit and she substituted her creative *spirit* with *spirits*. After five years of alcohol abuse, her canyon finally crumbled, stopping the flow of self-hatred and feelings of inadequacy. Though she had a mess to clean up, she also had a chance to rebuild the life she wanted. She had to try it on her own to testify that she tried everyone else's way and it didn't work for her.

As a result, our relationship was severed for the next 15 years. **That experience taught me that happiness is not about what happens in terms of outcomes. Happiness is about being purpose-filled in each moment, despite external circumstances.** When we are purpose-filled, we are aware of the unique reason we were put on this Earth and are striving to allow the Creator, Universe, God, or Spirit to fully express itself through us, as us. After managing her alcoholism with the help of Alcoholics Anonymous (AA), my mother regained her medical license and became an addictionologist. Through holistic healing, her goal is to prevent people from going down the path that she went down. Reflecting on the difference between the two positions, she said, "As an anesthesiologist I used to put people to sleep, but as an addictionologist, I bring people to life." She now knows that her purpose is to "minimize unnecessary pain." **Together, she and I are committed to creating the well-theist generation—a generation that believes wealth begins with wellness and self-knowledge.**

As her son, one of my goals is to create the Department of Motivated Vehicles, a community similar to AA for the millennial generation, by creating spaces like AA where people can find community, purpose, and a spiritual connection. Before AA, people are usually alone, feel purposeless, and are disconnected spiritually. AA is perhaps the best model of personal development in the world to date, but you shouldn't have to be an alcoholic to have access to community, purpose, and spiritual connection.

Like AA, I strongly believe personal development is not just personal—it's communal. Unfortunately, most vehicles in the world are driven with three empty seats. Life is a journey that is meant to be made with others and through that journey we are able to discover our unique purposes together. Today's notion of personal development is to buy a book, read it alone in your room, and claim that you've grown. However, if you've grown and the entire world around you stays the same, you are more likely to revert back to your old ways than if the world was changing with you.

Empty vehicles are a sign of emptiness, and people try to fill their lives with substitutes such as materialism, drugs, over eating, and gambling. Workaholism and successaholism are two additional issues that never get addressed but are equally dangerous to our well-being. A sense of purpose is the only thing that truly fulfills us. Purpose connects us to our Man-you-fact-urer, other people, and our original selves— the spiritual energy that existed before developing our physical form as human beings.

PROBLEMS AS FUEL

Problems are the fuel that powers your journey. They are the substance that your creative mind consumes to stay alive. Human beings have naturally been programmed to solve problems,

especially when it comes to matters of survival. Since the beginning of life, problems have always existed in the world. Imagine the problems the minds of the first living beings had to address. How do we stay warm in winter? How do we store food? How do we avoid disease? These are huge problems to solve. However, their ability to solve these problems is the reason we are here today. **Problems are fuel when we use them as motivation, but they are roadblocks when we allow them to stop us.**

Just like there is a perception that fuel is finite, there is a belief that we can have a problem-free world. Neither fuel nor problems are scarce resources. In the same way that our fuel sources have evolved from fire to steam to coal to fossil fuels to wind and solar power, new problems will evolve as we solve old ones. Every solution leads to new problems, which lead to new solutions, which lead to new problems, and so on and so on. It is a natural cycle. Nonetheless, each innovation leads to abundance, which often leads to overuse or abuse, and we're approaching a moment when our current fuel source is no longer efficient.

THE DEPARTMENT OF MOTIVATED VEHICLES & ALCOHOLICS ANONYMOUS

	Department of Motivated Vehicles (DMV)	Alcoholics Anonymous (AA)
Goal	Purpose-filled	Alcohol-free
Timing	Before addiction (preventative)	After addiction (reactive)
Elements	Supportive community, personal meaning, spiritual grounding	Supportive community, personal meaning, spiritual grounding
Partners	Closest friends walking similar paths	Other alcoholics who have walked similar paths
Process	8 Cylinders of Success	12 Steps Program
Relationship	Evaluate relationship to purpose and life	Evaluate relationship to alcohol and life
Frequency	Monthly	Every day
Story telling	Where I am and where I want to go (forward looking)	Where I was and where I am now (backward looking)
Requirement	Desire to change and say "yes" to purpose	Desire to change and say "no" to alcoholism
Basis	Purpose-based	Problem-based

Ideas that were once considered innovative are now harming the environment and it will take new innovation to solve the new problem.

We have approached solving the world's problems in the wrong way for a long time by adding fuel to the fire instead of letting existing flames burn themselves out. Believe it or not, fire is a natural part of forests and grassland ecology. In fact, foresters use a technique called controlled burns to stimulate the growth of some trees like sequoias. Likewise, there are creative ways to use the same substance that creates discomfort in our lives to create comfort and growth. The fuel that feeds the fire is not inherently bad; how we use the fuel is where we make mistakes.

Imagine that you are hitchhiking on the journey of life and you've made it to a gas station where you're waiting for a ride. Two cars pull up at the same time—one is going in the direction you want to go and the other one is going in the opposite direction. All you have is $10 to contribute. Which car's tank do you put your $10 into?

The answer seems straightforward, given this example. Ninety-nine percent of people would put their entire $10 into the car that is going their direction. **However, when it comes to fighting problems in the world today, instead of just creating the reality we want, we spend our energy pushing against the reality we don't want. If that which we resist persists, then that in which we invest progresses.** Some believe that by pushing the car not going in their direction backwards, they are advancing their own cause forward—when in reality, they haven't moved at all. Even if the $10 will only get you 10 miles in the direction you want to go versus pushing the other car backward 100 miles, 10 miles in the direction you want to go in is still a better investment.

Fuel is simply stored energy ready to set something in motion as it is transformed and burned off. Unfortunately, many people use fuel inefficiently. Instead of using our fuel to advance a particular movement in a positive direction, we fuel the fire of the movement going in the exact opposite direction. In these instances, the mileage per gallon is essentially zero. Anti-war, anti-abortion, anti-this and that movements are less efficient ways of reaching our goals than simply investing all of our energy in the direction we ultimately want our lives and the world to go. **Knowing what we don't want may stimulate you to imagine other possibilities, but simply pointing at what one *doesn't* want doesn't paint the picture of what they *do* want.**

Problems are just questions without answers. If there is no answer, then it is not a problem that should concern us. The problems we should care about are problems we genuinely believe have solutions. Some events are caused by the natural evolution of the world and thus we have no control over them. It is important to differentiate between what we have control over and what we don't and trust our Man-you-fact-urer to take care of what we can't control.

In order to find the right answers and soul-utions you have to ask the right questions. Some mechanics do this well. Based on a few symptoms, they know what questions to ask to reach the proper diagnosis. A mechanic treating for transmission failure won't ask questions related to the radiator. It is not economical for a mechanic to run every test possible on your car every time you take it in for a tune-up. Good mechanics ask good questions and then run the appropriate tests based on the information you provide. **The right answer to the wrong question won't get you where you want to go.**

Sometimes when things happen in our lives, we ask the question, "Why did this happen *to me*?" This question comes from the victim mentality—as if we're the only one in the world to whom tough things happen. If we're truly looking for insight, this is the wrong question to ask. **An alternative question to ask is, "Why did this happen *for me*?" This way of asking the question assumes that everything that happens *to us* happens *for us* and creates a unique experience of life that positions us to serve others.** The purpose of your journey thus far may be to help those behind you avoid taking the route you chose or experienced.

Some of the greatest change agents in the world understand the significance of this shift in consciousness and have used the things that happened to them to spark various movements (i.e. Free Hugs, Jenny Craig, AA). Our experience of life uniquely equips us to help those following in our path to make informed decisions if we are willing to share our authentic story. **The events in our lives that we think we need to hide because they hurt can be sources of fuel on our journey if we learn how to turn negative e-motion (emotional energy) into positive motion.**

Some of those movements have become profitable businesses. The problems that businesses solve are called consumer pain points or gain points. Apple solved the consumer need to access and manage their digital music by creating the iPod and iTunes. Google solved the consumer's need to find accurate information in the midst of the internet's growth and information explosion by creating PageRank. **A business that isn't solving a problem won't be in business for long. In the same way that your company was created to solve its customers' needs, you have been created to solve an outstanding need in**

someone's life directly or through an organization. All problems hurt people, thus all soul-utions must focus on helping people. Too much investment of thought, time, and money get poured into ideas that don't really help people in a substantial way.

The biggest problem in the world today is not global warming, population growth, or poverty. **Lack of creativity is the world's biggest problem. The 21st century is experiencing a Creativity Crisis.** Many of the world's environmental and economic issues are solvable. If we were creative enough to create the problem, then we can access the same source of creativity to solve the problem. To some people, some problems are too big to solve or life appears to just be a laundry list of problems. I agree that some problems are big and that there are a lot of problems, but the problem-solving mind has to out-think and out-create the problem-creating mind. **That is the process of elevating consciousness and the upward movement of our mind is how the world moves forward.**

Anyone committed to a cause genuinely believes that there is a solution. **We can either look to blame or look for answers, but we can't look both ways at the same time. Even if only a few people want to do the real work required to solve the problem, a few passionate opti-midsts (hopeful people who are able to see through the midst of uncertainty) is better than a few impassionate opti-midsts and a few pessimists.** A lot of pessimists think they're doing the world a favor by serving where nobody else is willing to serve. But if they don't believe in the possibility of change themselves, then they are actually hurting more than helping. A pessimist would be better off getting out of the way and doing what they love and believe in, rather than "sacrificing" themselves for a cause they don't believe in. Each of us serves the world best by emitting love through action and our passions. **Contrary to popular belief, service is not supposed to be sacrificial. Service should be a joyful act.**

We live in a world where people are more interested in *doing* good than *being* good. Ultimately, which will lead to a healthier global society? **We get distracted by *doing good* when the true call of humanity is *being good*, meaning that we're doing good all of the time.** Though it feels good to help someone, we should strive to help everyone by addressing the root causes of the problem so that the problem no longer exists. Many non-profit organizations say they are striving to obviate themselves through their work. Though I love the idea of trying to eliminate the need for one's self, I have yet to see a non-profit organization successfully do this. When a for-profit company obviates itself, it is called cannibalization. Cannibalization is defined as creating a new business line that makes an existing business less irrelevant because the new solution is far greater.

In the business world, service manifests itself as customer service. Customer service is the process of helping the customer identify their need, find the right solution, and provide ongoing support throughout the entire life of the product or engagement. The first and most important level of customer service is actually having a great product or service that solves a meaningful problem. The second step is customer relationship management—making sure that the customer is satisfied throughout the life of the product and loyal to the brand long-term.

Our entire life is supposed to be community service. Life was given to us freely therefore we should give of it free. Community service shouldn't be a derivative of our daily lives. Our life should be of service to the world. Many opportunities that sound good, volunteer and professional, will come to you throughout your life, but you have to ask yourself, "Where is my highest personal velocity?" Cleaning the beach on a Saturday morning sounds like a great thing to do for the environment, but if I know that my highest level of service to the world is writing this book or leading a Driving School for Life course, then that is what I should be doing rather than cleaning the beach.

Like our cars, we all have a lease on life. Eternal life costs life, but many of us haven't been making our payments. Shirley Chishom once said "Service to others is the rent you pay for your room here on Earth." True service is helping them solve their problems so that they can achieve their highest personal velocity.

THE SOURCE OF PROBLEMS

No one is immune to problems just as no car is immune to accidents, wear and tear, or maintenance. They come in many forms, including events that we experience, hear about, or witness. Considering all of the problems you have seen or faced, you must ask yourself, "Am I striving to address that which hurts me the most so that it doesn't hurt others?" The answer to this question can give you insight into what moves you. **One who has experienced a problem is usually the most equipped to help others overcome it.**

We are either moved to action as a result of something that has happened to us or we are moved by someone else's story about what happened to them. Either way, storytelling makes us feel connected to someone else's pain and we feel moved to do something. When you claim something as "my problem," you are taking ownership and committing yourself to changing it. You are adopting it into your consciousness and awareness and taking responsibility. The alternative is to say, "That's their problem."

Jacob L. Moreno is the founder of psychodrama—a form of human development, which explores, through dramatic action, the problems, issues, concerns, dreams, and highest aspirations of people, groups, systems and organizations. He once said, "By the group they were wounded. By the group they shall be healed." No man is an island unto himself. Every action has a reaction and the oneness of life binds us all together in such a way that one person's problem effects everyone.

TYPES AND EXAMPLES

Every human being wants to be needed and valued. However, most human beings try to avoid the void. Ironically, the void is where the untapped value is and where one must go to be valuable and create new value. I define the void as an unmet need or unsolved problem in the world that no one dares to solve. There are problems that already exist and then there are ones that you can create for yourself. Though most of the problems we experience are connected, they typically manifest in our lives in one of three ways: personal pains, social problems, and creative **quest-ions (problem so big that we must go on a quest to find the solution)**.

Personal pains: In life, we all experience, see, or hear about some sort of pain that negatively affects us. Personal pain is usually connected to larger social problems, but it means more to us because of the problem's proximity. Examples of personal pain include things like: disease (cancer, AIDS), disorders (ADD, blindness), or personal issues (low self-esteem, anger). Disease, disorders, and personal issues are the names given to these illnesses by a society that doesn't understand them or isn't willing to invest in solving them. The result is people suffering from these circumstances feeling alone and stigmatized. Fortunately, the e-motions can fuel the transformation of the *personal pain* into *public pleasure* (i.e. Lance Armstrong's Livestrong cancer movement) if the individual can use the negative experience as the impetus to unite others with a similar condition so that they feel supported and hopeful.

Social problems: Social problems are problems that usually existed in some form before we were born, but need to be addressed. Social problems include issues like: global warming, educational inequalities, and poverty. Like the kid that cleans up all of the toys even though he didn't take them all out, we may not have created these social problems, but we can adopt them and accept responsibility on behalf of previous and future generations. The magnitude of some social problems can lead to the bystander effect—a psychology term for a phenomenon in which someone is less likely to intervene in an emergency situation when other people are present and able to help than when he or she is alone. A lot of the world's problems are so big, we naturally assume that someone or something (i.e. government) is addressing them. And therefore, the individual stalls, when, in fact, the individual has the true power to impact the situation in the moment. To adopt a problem means to do what you can to dwarf these seemingly gigantic issues by assessing how you may be contributing knowingly, or unknowingly, and then doing your small part by adjusting any unjust habits while trusting that others are doing their part.

Creative quest-ions: Creative quest-ions are problems we create for ourselves to stimulate new thought and hopefully create value for others by improving their lives. As simple as they may be to create, Rubik's cube, Sudoku and crossword puzzles still exist because people like to be challenged. Examples of creative questions include Muhammad Yunus' pursuit of the quest-ion, "How can we make the poor bankable?" or Stephen Hawking's desire to answer the quest-ion, "How did the universe come to be?" Creative quest-ions usually come from someone's curiosity in the form of a quest-ion or hypothesis. Curiosity and imagination are the key ingredients of innovation. The Wright Brothers' quest to create the first airplane began with a quest-ion, or a problem so big that it became a lifelong quest to find the solution. Their quest-ion was simply stated, "Is it possible for man to fly?" They saw a gain point or opportunity for society to gain by being able to travel by sky—the inability to fly was not a personal pain nor a social problem beforehand. The Wright Brothers' creation has evolved into the massive airline industry and made national and international travel a possibility for many.

PERSONAL FUEL

Ironically, what you hate is what you're probably here to correct. If you aren't committed to correcting what you hate then you don't really hate it that much. What you hate gives some insight into what you love. We usually

EXAMPLES OF PROBLEMS

PERSONAL PAINS	SOCIAL PROBLEMS	CREATIVE QUEST-IONS
» Low self-esteem » Anger » Materialism » Insecurity » Illiteracy » Bi-polar » AIDS » Alcoholism » Anemia » Depression	» Underemployment » Unemployment » Poverty » Racism » Hunger » Foster Care System » Educational Inequalities » Gender Discrimination »Unnecessary disease » Environmental Abuse » Obesity » Cancer » Aids » Gang Violence » War	» Muhammad Yunus: How do help extricate the poor from poverty and change the world's perception of them as unbankable? » Steve Jobs: How do I make digital music and other media part of people's everyday experience? » Henry Ford: How do I make a car affordable to the common man?

love the opposite of what we hate (if there is an opposite). Hate is the strongest negative energy in the world and we have the creative challenge of converting that negative energy into positive energy. Our commitment to solving problems is rooted in love just like our passions, however, it is our love of the alternative possibilities that moves us. **Whereas our passions hopefully *inspire* forever, we hope that the problems we care about *expire* forever. We do our passions *just because* and we adopt *problems because it's just*.**

The personal pain that we think we need to hide is usually the thing that makes us most powerful. Alcoholics

113

Anonymous has done an amazing job of turning a social stigma into opportunities to allow someone to find meaning through service by giving sober alcoholics the opportunity to sponsor new members who have recently decided to stop drinking. The worst feeling in the world is to feel like you are alone and without help. We are all dealing with hidden problems we feel are unique to us, but if we were vocal about them, we would likely find that people close to us who we never would have imagined actually share the same problem. In this scenario, we all lose by missing out on an opportunity to connect deeply with each other and help each other heal.

The problems we share can be binding forces among people, and as we overcome our problems together, new ones arise. Our passions also lead us to new problems. As we master our passions, we start to create new challenges for ourselves. Researchers do this all of the time. "How can I take what I know now and use it to solve a problem or create new knowledge that may help the world?" This type of thinking doesn't have to be limited to the academic world. Of all of the 8 Cylinders of Success to align, the a-line-meant of your passions with a problem you care about is the most important because it allows you to do what you love while addressing something you hate, which is double the motivation of someone doing just one of the two.

PROFESSIONAL FUEL

In our professional lives, problems create the space for industry-wide opportunities or gain points. No matter what organization you're in or your position in the organization, it is important to know what problem you're solving, how valuable a solution to that problem is to your company, and

COMPANY PROFILE:
PROBLEMS & UNDER ARMOUR

Under Armour, a sportswear company, was started in 1996 by former University of Maryland football player Kevin Plank. Under Armour is the originator of performance apparel—gear engineered to keep athletes cool, dry and light throughout the course of a game, practice or workout.

Plank simply took a problem he was personally experiencing and set out to make a superior product that worked with your body to regulate temperature and enhance performance. As a college football player for the University of Maryland, Plank was known as the "sweatiest guy on the football field" and would change in and out of multiple cotton t-shirts during the span of practice or a game to stay dry and comfortable. Instead of pursuing his football career after graduating from the University of Maryland, he set out to find synthetic materials to prototype sportswear that would solve this problem for thousands of athletes like him. From Plank's problem and that first prototype, Under Amour was born.

Since starting business in 1996, Under Amour has demonstrated amazing growth. In the midst of the worst economic downturns in the United States, Under Armour reported a 20% top line growth for 2008 with revenues of $725.2M and operating income of $76.9M. The company is expanding into other lines of business like shoes and new markets such as college sports and the military.

what dashboard number shows that you're doing a great job. For an operations manager, their problem may be how to improve quality control and reduce waste. For an HR representative, it may be employee retention. For a CEO, their problem may be instilling a strong company culture reflected by quarterly results and employee satisfaction. On the customer-side, one of the greatest metrics to gauge how well your company or department is solving problems in the marketplace is your Net Promoter Score which is a customer loyalty metric that captures how many other people your customers are telling about your service. If your product or service works great, then your customers will openly share it with their friends and word of mouth is the best form of marketing. (At this time, please feel free to tell someone about this book if you like it so far!)

The business problems that have stemmed from "What if" quest-ions have probably led to some of the most innovative solutions and companies to date. "What if" quest-ions apply to personal problems, social problems, and creative quest-ions. "What if" quest-ions challenge widely held assumptions about an industry, technology, or customers. The Wright Brothers' challenged the assumption that "Man can't fly" by dedicating their creative energy to make the first airplane. Muhammad Yunus challenged the assumption that the poor were not bankable and proved it through the Grameen Bank. Henry Ford challenged the assumption that only the elite would be able to afford cars by creating the assembly line to make production more efficient so that his employees could buy cars too. Other game-changing, technologies include TiVo, iPhone, iPod, and Netflix. Our assumptions and fear of releasing those assumptions is often what sustains the personal problems and social problems in the world. But creative quest-ions and those on the quest to solve them uproot our assumptions about ourselves and our relationships to other people and things, which removes former limits and thus create a pathway for new innovations.

In order to adopt a problem requires selflessness. Selflessness and service are the keys that separate what Rick Warren calls the "purpose driven life" from just a career. Everyone who makes money is solving some sort of problem or pain. Mechanics solve car problems. Dentists solve teeth problems. Google solves information search problems. Even beggars solve people's desire to give or release guilt.

What problem do you feel equipped with the experience, passion, and skills to solve? **You must tap into your entrepre-new-real (imaginative ability to create new realities) spirit and create a new reality as entrepre-new-ers (those creating new realities through a new organization) or intrapre-new-ers (those creating new realities within an existing organization)**. The world's best entrepreneurs and many of company profiles throughout this book demonstrate that the most powerful ideas come when you are able to match your passion with a problem to create a powerful product or service. When you tap into your uniqueness, authentic and innovative ideas are destined to arise. **To change something is to create new avenues to an existing destine-nation or new ones, dis-covering a better way to make an even better way.**

PROBLEM & PASSION BEFORE PROFESSION

Before choosing a career path, you should evaluate your problems and passions first without any career path in mind. Once you have clarity about what problems and move you and what you are passionate about, then you should explore professions that may be in line with them and that will allow you to address and exercise them full-time. If you can align your passions with a problem that you deeply care about, then you're in a better position than having just one of the two. People say they want to be things like a doctor or a lawyer without truly understanding the true nature and activities of the job, the problems they solve, or the passions they require. If you are interested in being a doctor and discover that you're passionate about healing, then great. But don't say that you want to be a doctor without knowing the passions, activities, and feelings associated with the work.

PASSION + PROBLEM = PRODUCT OR SERVICE

PERSON	PASSION +	PROBEM =	PRODUCT OR SERVICE
Yunus	Studying Economics	Poverty	Micro-finance and the Grameen Bank
Kevin Plank	Playing football	Perspiration	Under Amour
Lance Armstrong	Cycling	Cancer	Livestrong
Bono	Making music	Poverty, AIDS, foreign debt	one campaign, Live 8, Red Campaign
Sergey Brin & Larry Page	Computer science	Information explosion	Google.com search engine
Oprah	Broadcasting, media	Lack of empowering entertainment for women by women	Harpo Networks

PROBLEM + PASSION = PROFESSION

PROBLEMS +	PASSIONS =	PROFESSION
Unhealthiness, inequitable healthcare, AIDS, cancer	Healing, working with hands, helping, learning about anatomy, solving problems, promoting health, communicating with people	Doctor
Injustice, discrimination	Litigating, negotiating, fighting for justice, writing, debating	Lawyer
Ignorance, unequal opportunities, wasted potential	Public speaking, sharing, creating, learning, inspiring, being with kids	Teacher
Economic disparities, poverty, inefficiency, various needs in society	Creating, building (organizations), planning, strategizing, leading, working in teams, making money, employing people, giving others opportunities to grow and be creative	Businessperson
Inefficiency, pollution	Working with hands, problem solving, building, improving society, making life easier for others, creating	Engineer

CONCLUSION

We are programmed to problem-solve and within every human being is a soul-ution to someone else's problem. Every problem needs a soul-ution just as much as every solution needs a problem. It's a symbiotic relationship. **By**

focusing on soul-utions, we ensure that we're not changing the tires on vehicle without an engine. It would be frustrating to make in invention and then be unable to find a problem it can solve for others. Likewise, it is frustrating to have a problem, know there is a solution out there somewhere, and be unable to find it.

If everyone stated what problem they wanted to focus on solving and we took a global inventory, we would have enough people to solve the problems of the world ten times over. In order to serve authentically and find soul-utions, you must internalize the problem as if it is yours, knowing that when anyone falls short of their potential, so do you. **When you externalize problems, then the solution lives outside of you and is therefore out of your control.** Your creative mind has the power to create whatever reality it wants, but you also need the courage to pursue that reality for yourself and others despite fear of failure. As we will explore in the next chapter, every meaningful problem we adopt could change the lives of many people.

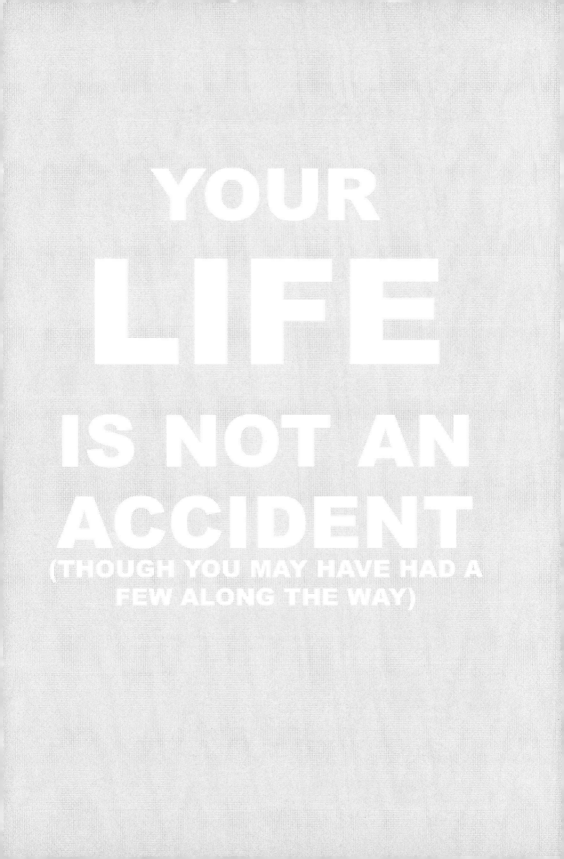

YOUR LIFE IS NOT AN ACCIDENT (THOUGH YOU MAY HAVE HAD A FEW ALONG THE WAY)

INNER TERM-OIL

Directions: Think of problems you see in the lives of your family, friends, company, and community. Complete the following charts for your personal and professional life to explore the problems that are currently present in your life and around you. Observe any patterns in the types of problems you notice.

Personal Pains & Gain Points:

Problems I have face in my life:...

....

Problems others close to me are facing:................................

....

Social Problems:

Social problems that make me mad/sad:................................

....

Causes I've donated to or volunteered for:............................

....

Creative Questions

If I had one wish, I would put an end to the problem of:.........

....

Business ideas I've thought but not acted on:.........................

....

Professional Pain & Gain Points:

The 3 biggest problems I hear our customers mention about *their business* are:

1...

2...

3...

The 3 biggest problems I hear our customers mention about *our products/services* are:

1...

2...

3...

The 3 biggest problems I hear my colleagues mention about *our company* are:

1...

2...

3...

MOVE-MEANT

Where The Rubber Meets The Road

Below are specific actions you can do in the next 30 days to align your life a little bit more with the personal and professional problems you care about most.

Personal: Think about personal challenges, fears, physical disabilities, weaknesses, insecurities, childhood events, or addictions that you have overcome and dedicate time to solving the problem for others or supporting people currently facing the problem.

Professional: Create a proposal to address the problem that you think would create the most value for your company if solved and submit it to your boss to see if you can allocate time to solving it.

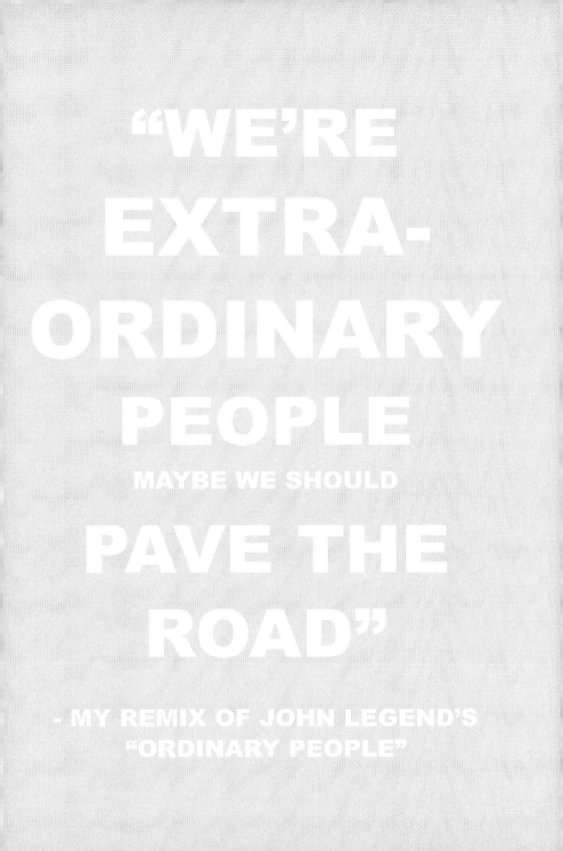

"WE'RE EXTRA-ORDINARY PEOPLE MAYBE WE SHOULD PAVE THE ROAD"

- MY REMIX OF JOHN LEGEND'S "ORDINARY PEOPLE"

PEOPLE »
YOUR MOTOR

THE PURPOSE OF THIS CHAPTER IS TO:

- Identify who you want to serve, how, and why
- Identify how to serve more through serving yourself

GUIDING QUEST-IONS:

Personal: Who moves you to want to serve them and in what way?

Professional: Who is my company's target market or customer? Who do I serve to ensure that the end customer receives quality service?

QUOTES:

"You can have everything in life you want as long as you will help enough other people get what they want!"
— Zig Ziglar

"A lot of people are waiting for Martin Luther King or Mahatma Gandhi to come back—but they are gone. We are it. It is up to us. It is up to you."
— Marian Wright Edelman

JOHN WALSH'S PEOPLE: ADAM WALSH & OTHERS' FAMILIES

One of the greatest examples of one person's story altering the lives of many comes from the Walsh family and the murder of their 6-year-old son, Adam Walsh, in 1981. Despite their tragedy, John and Revé Walsh used their experience as fuel to establish the Adam Walsh Child Resource Center, which eventually merged with the National Center for Missing & Exploited Children (NCMEC), which they co-founded in 1984.

In 1988, John Walsh became the host of *America's Most Wanted* with the purpose of profiling and assisting law enforcement in the apprehension of fugitives wanted for various crimes. *America's Most Wanted* is the longest-running program of any kind in the history of the Fox Network and led to the capture of more than 1,000 criminals during its 20-year history.

It took more than 27 years to close the case of Adam Walsh due to missing evidence, yet despite their agonizing wait the Walsh family still remains dedicated to preventing what happened to them from happening to other families across America. In response to an interview on the Early Show, "You've made it part of your life's mission to make sure that what happened to your son doesn't happen again. In the end, can you walk away from this?" John Walsh answered "It's become our life mission. You know how life takes you in the strangest ways. *America's Most Wanted* is certainly my passion. 21 years we've caught 1,000 plus fugitives in 135 countries…We've suffered firsthand the problems with not having a National DNA Database." Walsh succinctly captures his purpose, principles (# of fugitives caught), passions, and problems in this short. His clarity and a-line-meant with the first four cylinders helps keep him motivated to relentlessly address children's safety issues every day.

MY PEOPLE: GENERATION 'WHY'—THE MILLENNIALS

My motor is my mom and the millennial generation—defined as the high-potential, socially-aware, and tech savvy generation. Though my mother is not a millennial, she is my **motor-vator (a person who motivates you on your journey).** She inspires my commitment to the millennial generation because I want millennials to have the support systems and professional passion that she didn't have in the same way that Walsh family is supporting other families with their work.

The millennial generation includes anyone born between 1980 and 2000. We're also known as the YouTube Generation or Generation Y. There are over 57 million millennials in the United States. We are coming of age in an unprecedented time with the election of the first diverse president of the United States, extreme economic turmoil, the rise of social entrepreneurship, and the expansion of social networks among other trends. As a result of the dynamic changes in the world, we are characterized as always online, text messagers and bloggers, culturally-diverse, and socially-conscious.

While older generations think that this generation has it easier than generations of the past, being a millennial comes with its own challenges. With the rise of globalization as captured in Thomas Friedman's *The World Is Flat*, millennials have to compete in a global marketplace whereas previous generations simply had to outperform the student or employee sitting next to them. Today, even a 4.0 isn't enough because the education system isn't evolving as quickly as the world is changing. As a result, many millennials are dealing with the quarter life crisis, a challenging time of insecurity, confusion, disappointment, loneliness, and sometimes depression. In order to navigate these times and stay motivated, people will have to be self-motivated, creative, entrepreneurial, quick learners, problem-solvers, and have strong interpersonal skills. The world is evolving at such a pace that there is no road map to follow for success and therefore it must be created by our imagination and intentions.

I believe that the millennial generation has the potential to be the greatest generation to ever live. Philosopher and author Frantz Fanon writes, "Each generation must out of relative obscurity discover its mission, fulfill it, or betray it." My goal is to help the millennial generation discover and fulfill its mission and purpose. My pioneers—Tony Robbins, Oprah Winfrey, and Marcus Buckingham—are serving Baby Boomers like my parents. Serving the generation before them were the likes of Wayne Dwyer, Jim Rohn, and Jack Canfield. My focus is to position myself as the leading personal development guru for the millennial generation.

PEOPLE AS MOTOR

People are the driving force behind our lives and work in the same way that a motor moves a vehicle. They motor-vate us on our journeys through who and how they move others and how we could possibly move them forward. As we construct the vehicle of our lives we need identify who we are designing it for and how many people.

My vehicle would look like a Mitsubishi Fuso dump truck because I am great at recycling and repurposing wasted potential. My choice is motivated by my commitment to move masses of millennials whom I think have the potential to be the greatest generation to ever live, yet many are currently underemployed or unemployed. The vehicle of my life carries millennials and organizations that employ them or serve them from a state of underutilized potential to full potential.

Similar to a taxi cab, people step into our lives, tell us where they are trying to go, and we do our best to help them get there as safely and quickly as possible. We use our GPS or purpose to help them navigate areas of life that they are unfamiliar with. From their perspective, they are just passengers in our vehicle, as we help them get from point A to point B or one state of their lives to the next. But without passengers, taxi cabs are not able to make their highest contribution to the world. **One of the greatest gifts you can give someone is the opportunity to help. When people are given the opportunity to serve, they feel valuable. Therefore, one of the greatest gifts someone can give you is the opportunity to serve them with your greatest gifts.**

Seeing and being part of the positive movement in other people's lives is what motivates us. **The vehicles of our lives should help people get to where they want to go faster, safer, and easier.** We need other people just as much as other people need us. No man is an island unto him or herself. Together, we make up a mass transportation system that moves the world forward. Traffic in one area of humanity affects all humanity, but it can be mitigated if we coordinate and carpool through life and help each other.

Unfortunately, most people drive through life alone. Most cars are four-seaters, yet they only transport one person a majority of the time. Imagine if everyone just committed their entire life to helping four people succeed. What if you were responsible for creating a 4-person carpool to help others as you advanced along your journey? There are only cases of few individuals serving many because so many serve so few.

The commitment to serve a particular group of comes before the actual passengers. It is important to note that the commitment usually arises first and that the physical process of moving people forward simply supports an inner motivation that is already present. Whether in a for-profit or non-profit organization this holds true. An entrepreneur is motor-vated by a problem that they see is negatively affecting people and sets out to help in hopes of then finding people who like their solution to the present problem. It's futile for anyone or any organization to dedicate energy to problems that aren't affecting people.

Your economic engine depends on knowing who you serve and how. It will only work if you are working for people. Each of us should have stories to tell of people whose lives we have change in the same way that we can tell stories of people who have changed our lives. This should be our motor-vation. Without it we are stuck. Ask yourself "Who do I or want to create value for?" "Who is in my carpool?" "How many seats do I have?" "Where can I take people?" **Identifying who values your gifts and allows you to use them freely will result in an infinite amount of motivation so that your engine never burns out.**

THE SOURCE OF PEOPLE

As we develop our identity during childhood, one of the first expansions of the individual self comes as a result of our family. Our first names make us unique, but we realize that our last names unite us to a larger family tree. At that age, family is solely biological, but over time, family transcends biology. As we mature, situations like college, death, and careers may separate us from our biological families and we are forced to create new families wherever we go.

We only act in the best interest of the people we are serving when we believe that they are like family or part of ourselves in some way. Therefore, a good place to begin to identify the people you want to serve is wherever your definition of family ends. The destiny of the people you choose to serve must be intertwined with your own. Successfully serving whom you love will increase your capacity to love and an increased capacity to love allows one to expand their definition of family by unconditionally loving others. They say, "the heart is where the home is," so whom you choose to serve plays a big part in where you choose to serve as well.

It wasn't until college that I learned the true meaning of service. Through the UCLA Community Programs Office, I served as a peer advisor to 30 young men and women from sixth grade to high school. Even some of my classmates and colleagues came to me for advice and considered me their mentor. Through serving my community, I discovered who valued me and why. I learned that I had a unique ability to communicate to the younger generation through metaphor and teach without them knowing that they're being taught through creating collective experiences and curriculum. I

133

found my audience—people who valued my opinion and listened to me. Serving others is how I developed my commitment to the millennial generation and my awareness of my passions, problems, and other cylinders of success.

PERSONAL MOTOR

Service always begins with self. Taking the time find to purpose is a form of self-service. **If the self is not properly pre-served (self-inspected before trying to move others), then it cannot serve others to its full capacity. This doesn't mean that you have to be perfect to serve.** In fact, your imperfections allow you to serve even better because your awareness of your own areas for growth ensures your compassion for those you are serving. **Personal development isn't about adding to or subtracting from what you already have. You have everything you need within you. Like your car, you simply need maintenance to fine-tune yourself so that you can be of service to others to the best of your ability.** A broken-down city bus is of no service to residents who rely on public transportation if it can't move. Perfection is not required to serve authentically, however it is essential to be in tune with your own problems and shortcomings.

Most people would call service to one's self selfish. **Service to self is only selfish when your definition of self is limited to yourself. Once you expand your definition of self, you will begin to see that your every action serves the self.** The only way to love thy neighbor as thyself is to recognize that they are part of your larger self and thus treat them like you would treat yourself. We consciously and unconsciously seek what we think is best for us (even if it ultimately isn't). When we are making a decision for ourselves, our intention is usually in search of the greatest good for us. Likewise, you can only serve with a pure heart if you truly believe that whom you are serving is a part of yourself. Any other type of service is considered charity.

The current concept of charity implies that the destiny of the giver and receiver are not intertwined. There is the charitable giver and there is "them," the receiver. **When the giver does not see themselves in the receiver, then the giver cannot possibly have the receiver's best interest in mind for we only seek the genuine greatest good when we are seeking for self.** As a litmus test, we can always ask ourselves, "Am I seeking to make that which makes me happiest available to anyone who wants it?" If the answer to this question is "no," that means that we are happy with our relative position in society and are only willing to give of ourselves to the extent that our position is preserved. True service seeks to advance change by sacrificing the individual self for the advancement of the greater collective self, which in the end hopefully puts the individual in a better position that he was on his own.

The self expands in many different ways but true service is still self-serving. The self is commonly defined biologically, culturally, organizationally, nationally, or spiritually. After transcending the individual definition of self, self is typically defined biologically by our immediate families. Some call this "my blood." "I Love New York" shirts and American flags are classic example of the national self. We experience the organizational self every day when employees say "my company" even when they aren't shareholders. Occasionally, you will hear someone say I have to take care of "my people" or "my community." This refers to a cultural or spiritual affiliation. Whenever someone begins using the word "my"

without talking solely about him or herself, their definition of self is expanding.

These different expansions of self act upon us simultaneously and affect our identity. They support our desire to be a part of something greater and give us opportunities to expand from our individual definition of self. However, losing one's self to the larger self can be detrimental if the individual forgets their unique purpose within the larger purpose. When considering whom we want to serve and why, we must look at how we define who we are. Of all the things we use to differentiate ourselves from each other, our purpose is the only thing truly unique about us.

People range from wanting to impact their immediate family to wanting to impact the entire world. The number of people touched does not necessarily measure impact. Whether someone impacts two or two million people, their impact is equal. **To me, account-ability means *accounting* for what we know we have the *ability* to do.** Since only we know our true potential, the real question is whether or not the individual feels like they did all they could for who they could.

PROFESSIONAL MOTOR

People always say that they want to work for themselves, but regardless if we have a boss or not, we are always working for others. The only way to create value and capture some as income is to create it for others first. Though a beginning entrepreneur may not have anyone to report to, they are working for their current and future customers.

COMPANY PROFILE:
PEOPLE & APPLE

With its revolutionary 1984 NFL Super Bowl commercial release, it was clear that Apple stood for the "other" computer user. Fast-forwarding almost 25 years later, Apple launches its Mac vs. PC advertising campaign. Their Mac vs. PC commercial juxtaposes a young hip millennial against an old corporate pot belly guy with glasses. Apple is positioning itself to be the leading hardware and software provider for the independent computer user, especially creative professionals: artists, editors, writers, photographers, musicians, videographers, and young entrepreneurs. Though Macs can be pricey, they have a suite of hardware and software with iTunes, the iPhone, and the iPod that synch together seamlessly. As the iPod and iPhone market continues to expand, it will surely lead to more direct sales of Mac desktops and laptops.

In addition to superior products, Apple offers superior customer service in-store and via phone. Walking into an Apple store feels like you're in a video gaming conference with workshops on how to get a bite out of your Apple computer, 1-on-1 support at the Genius Bar, and hundreds of Apple products to play with. In the 2008 American Customer Satisfaction Index, Apple scored a rating of 85%, an industry high, increasing 8% from the year before, putting them 10 full percentage points ahead of their nearest competitor in a time where customer service ratings were declining. Apple knows whom they are serving and who they are not and has never been ashamed of their choice.

Whether you're an employee for a for-profit, non-profit, the government, or self, the goal is to make the world a better place for more people. Serving one another unconditionally is one of our primary reasons for being. Instead of seeing ourselves as one, we have a tendency to divide and differentiate. We define each other in many ways: gender, class, race, education level, common problem, or age. Regardless of how we define a group of people, we cannot authentically serve them until "serving them" becomes "serving myself through serving others." We must see ourselves in those we serve, meaning that thoughts of inferiority and superiority dissipate and the situation is seen as a simple resource (intellectual, social, or financial capital) imbalance that can be addressed through exchange.

In business, the people served are called customers or clients. Businesses are systems set up to help someone or a group of people do something better, faster, or cheaper than they could do on their own. Any company should be able to give you case studies of how they moved a real customer from point A to point B in their lives. That's how true value is created and captured. Companies hire consulting firms and contractors for the same reason that individuals hire a personal trainer or life coach. They can help people move toward their goals at a higher velocity than the people can on their own.

Business enables some of the value being created to be captured so that the value creation process can sustain itself. Great companies innovate and open new markets by focusing on solving huge problems real people face instead just focusing on where the current flow of currency is the highest. Sometimes the money isn't where the market is initially, but business always gravitates to where value is being created. When you neglect opportunities to serve who you want, you are neglecting yourself, your purpose, and financial opportunities. You should serve whom you feel naturally inclined to serve and decline to serve whom you don't want to. Where you feel naturally inclined to serve is likely where the greatest opportunities for you are in terms of value and impact.

In many cases, we end up creating value for people who don't share our values. There are many companies that I would find it hard to give my time and energy to because I don't believe that their products or services are really helping people live well-thier lives. It may also be hard for me to work for an investment bank if I was unaware of whom I was actually making wealthier with my time and skills. What if they invest the money I make for them into lifestyles, companies, or organizations that have missions that contradict the world I envision? This would be like slitting my own tires. When you think critically about who you are creating value for, you should consider how much you share values with your customer and how aligned their vision of the world is with your own.

WORK IS COMMUNITY SERVICE

Service is unconditional love in practice. There is no income, age, ethnic, or academic requirements to love or to serve. Service is the breeding ground for purposeseekers because it shows one that even without qualifications or money, their life can have a positive impact on many lives. **Through service, one gets to exercise their creativity, develop their compassion, and display their capabilities without fear of failure, judgment, or loss. With fear set aside, the individual has the freedom to do what they want, how**

they want, for whom they want, and for however long they want. The cost of service is nothing more than time, energy, and love, which are all unlimited resources given to you freely by your Man-you-fact-urer.

Service has no start-up cost. From the stories that I've heard, many successful entrepreneurs began their companies by simply serving others first. The story of the great-tasting Potbelly Sandwich Works company found on their website is a great example of how genuine service led to dollar signs:

"Potbelly Sandwich Works began in 1977 as a small antique store run by a nice young couple. Despite the fast-paced, never-a-dull-moment world of antique dealing, the couple decided to bolster their business by making sandwiches for their customers. What began as a lark, turned out to be a stroke of genius. Soon, people who couldn't care less about vintage glass doorknobs were stopping by to enjoy special sandwiches and homemade desserts in this unusual atmosphere."

Today, Potbelly Sandwich Works has more than 200 stores nationwide. Usually, the story happens as follows: Person A offers their time for free because they see an opportunity to help Person B. Person B loves what Person A does so much that they tell Person C. Person C reaches out the Person A and then a business is born. If you can manage to positively impact lives without a dime, how many lives will you be able to impact with a dollar?

When we talk about serving people, we tend to think non-profit, yet every product you've bought or experience you've paid for is a service. **Service is not just a non-profit or**

volunteer word. Businesses serve people every day, hence the name customer service. There are for-profit corporations that are solving real needs that help the service recipients, whom they call customers, reach their personal and organizational goals. **Once companies identify the type of person who values their products or services most, that demographic becomes their target market.**

A new company observes the competitive market and identifies where **non-customers (people who would buy but aren't buying)** exist and explores how current customers could be served better than they are today. The goal of any business or organization is to expand its ability to create value for a specific target market and then capture some of that value financially. In the same way, it is impossible for us to serve everyone in the world, so we should be clear about our personal target market—the people we add the most value for based on who we are and what we do best—and focus on serving them.

CONCLUSION

The types of people you want to serve can come from many sources. The Walsh's story and my story are personal stories that hit home hard. You may be motivated by operational inefficiencies that cause mid-size companies to fail. Regardless of your story's source, you must define whom you want to serve and go where they are since that is where you will add the most value. Defining whom you want to serve is not limiting—it is empowering. Rather than trying to disperse your energy over many people and lessening the chance of true impact, clarity on your "customer" focuses your energy, which increases your likelihood of success. Success comes from many small wins whereas long shot hopes are based on luck.

The entire world you see is built off relationships—chemical bonds, family ties, cause and effect. At the end of the day it is all about transforming how people relate to one another, and your purpose is the most powerful way to relate. **If you're not transforming relationships and how people relate to one another, you're not changing the world. Who you serve is equally important to how you serve them with your passions.** In addition to finding and aligning with your own purpose, you know that you are authentically serving others when you are helping them discover and align their lives with their purposes. We are all on parallel journeys and our journeys are dependent on one another. One person can't reach their full potential unless everyone is at their full potential. **The goal of life isn't to get others to serve you —it's for you to figure out whom you can serve.**

AUTO-BIOGRAPHY

Directions: Write the auto-biography of whom you want to serve. Address where they are on their journey when you meet, how you want to serve them, and where they end up as a result of your service. Create the character or pull from a true story.

My name is (Customer Name)...and I was initially in a state of ....
....
....

Before I met (Your Name).., I was [] stuck & not going anywhere [] broken & not going fast enough [] lost & not going the right way. On my own, it was impossible for me to reach my desired state, which is
....
....

(Your Name) .... helped me get there by (What you did)...
....
....
....

As a result of his/her contribution, it is now possible for me to
....
....

This profound change in my life allows me to use my vehicle to positively impact (Who they serve)....................................
....

MOVE-MEANT

Where The Rubber Meets The Road

Below are specific actions you can do in the next 30 days to align your life a little bit more with the people you want to serve personally and professionally.

Personal: Reach out to someone who fits the profile of the person you wrote the auto-biography about and really try to understand their roadblocks, their goals, and how they think you can best serve them. They could be a friend, mentee, or family member among others. Dedicate the next month to help them create the success story they want to have.

Professional: Arrange to take whomever you're serving on a daily basis at work out to lunch and really get to know who they are, their goals, and what is preventing them from achieving their professional goals. This could be your boss, a client, or your colleagues. Dedicate the next month to help them create the success story they want to have.

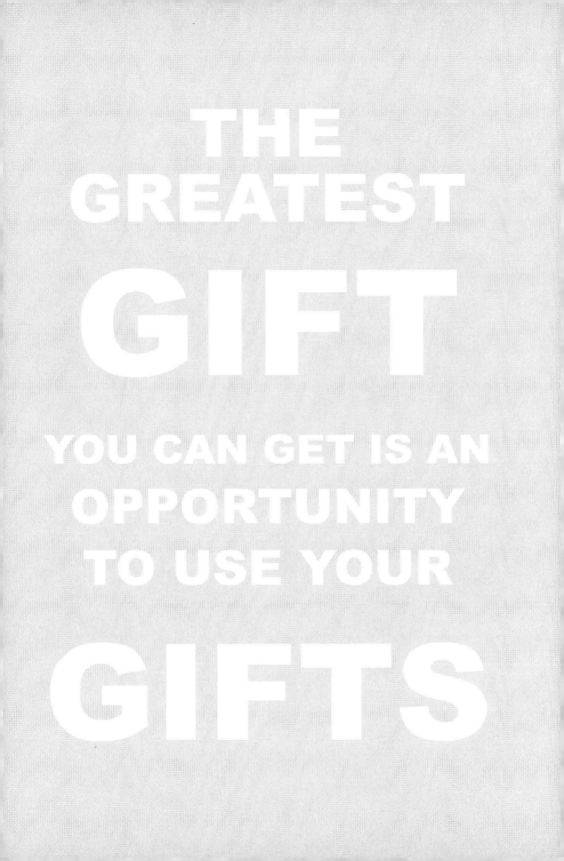

THE
GREATEST

GIFT

YOU CAN GET IS AN
OPPORTUNITY
TO USE YOUR

GIFTS

PART 2: WHERE AM I GOING?

In Part 2 we will explore the question "Where am I going?" Part 2 is about visioning and forward thinking into existence that which is absent in the world but will only come forth because of your courage and clarity to create it. Given that you know where you are now, the second step to planning any trip is deciding where you want to go. Once you have point A and point B, you can design a road map that allows you to create an infinite amount of routes and destine-nations along the way. By creating new destine-nations, we expand the possibilities in the world for everyone as opposed to being limited by a pre-existing menu of options that other people have already traveled. We will explore the last 4 Cylinders of Success: positioning, pioneers, picture, and possibility.

.

POSITIONING »
YOUR LANE

THE PURPOSE OF THIS CHAPTER IS TO:

- Identify what skill or subject you want to seek to master
- Create a personal practice plan based on what you want to master

GUIDING QUEST-IONS:

Personal: What do I want to be #1 in the world at?

Professional: What business or industry does my company want to establish itself as a leader? What is my career positioning me to be great at doing?

QUOTES:

"The purpose of the positioning statement is to be borne in mind and conformed to in everything you say and do."
— Drayton Bird

"If your position is everywhere, your momentum is zero."
— William Lipscomb

149

LIL WAYNE'S POSITIONING: BEST RAPPER ALIVE

I remember thinking I was a Hot Boy when the Hot Boy$ released their first album on Cash Money Records in the summer of 1999. At the time, Lil Wayne was just the little guy in the four-man group and I remembered him for his youth and the sound effects he included in his raps. After their *Guerilla Warfare* album and the release of his first solo album that same year, Lil Wayne fell off my radar for a while. It wasn't until 2006 that my youngest brother brought Lil Wayne back to my attention with his Carter II album and his wide array of mixtapes and features.

On *Tha Carter II*, Lil Wayne was bold enough to create a song titled "Best Rapper Alive." Since hearing that song, it has been clear to me and the world through his words and actions that Lil Wayne was positioning himself for that crown, especially with Jay-Z and Eminem in retirement. *Tha Carter III* was the most anticipated album of 2008. Between its release and the December 2005 release date of *Tha Carter II*, Lil Wayne went to work. During that two-and-half-year period, he released more than 200 songs on various mixtapes and as a featured artist on other artists' albums. As of now, his song count is almost at 600 while Jay-Z, his pioneer, is only around 400 songs.

In a 2008 interview with *The Source* magazine, Lil Wayne shared his perspective on being the best when he said "You should feel like you're the best with anything you do, whoever you are. I just happen to rap so I said I'm the best rapper. If you don't think you're the best at something what are you doing it for?"

Nobody in hip-hop (and perhaps nobody in the world) was working as hard as Lil Wayne during this period of time. His commitment to excellence on *Tha Carter III* created momentum that led to a high-grossing concert tour and record-breaking album sales resulting in annual revenue of $57,441,334, according to the Billboard charts. *Tha Carter III's* opening day sales figures were approximately 423,000, and the album sold 1,005,545 units in its first week in the United States. With its first week sales, it is the largest first week sales for any album in 2008 in the United States and the first album of any genre to reach a million in one week since 50 Cent's *The Massacre* in 2005. The album went on to sell over three million copies, but most important, Lil Wayne successfully transformed everyone's image of him in the post-Hot Boys era through hard work, discipline, and practice. In an interview on P. Diddy's blog, Lil Wayne said, "I'm in the studio, on set, or on stage...anything else is uncivilized." If the music industry wasn't changing so quickly, perhaps we could use album sales to compare Lil Wayne's achievement to Jay-Z, Eminem, The Notorious B.I.G., and 2Pac, but we can't. Given the times, I still think it's fair to say that he is on their level.

Lil Wayne has modeled his entire career after Jay-Z's. Not only do they both share the last name Carter, but even other little things overlap down to how Lil Wayne's Young Money Records logo looks like the logo on the New York Yankees cap Jay-Z regularly wears. Jay-Z acknowledged Lil Wayne on *Tha Carter III* song "Mr. Carter" when he said,"...as I share/Mic time with my heir/Young Carter/Go farther/Go further/Go harder/Is that not why we came?/And if not, Then why bother?" By the time Lil Wayne reaches the stage of life that his pioneer Jay-Z is at currently, he has the potential to transform the entire music industry. In 2009, he released his first rock album called *Rebirth* in an attempt to first, challenge himself as a musician and, secondly, expand his market. Jay-Z has paved roads in music by creating the *Collision Course* album with Linkin Park and becoming the first hip-hop headliner at Glastonbury 2008, the traditionally all-rock British music festival. Lil Wayne is taking what his pioneer has done and running with it. Now that he has proven himself to be one of the best rappers alive, perhaps he is shooting for the best musician alive in the company of Michael Jackson and Madonna.

MY POSITIONING: WORLD'S #1 PURPOSEFINDER

I was the only junior on the junior varsity basketball team. JV teams are usually only for freshmen and sophomores. On top of that, I wasn't even a starter. Nonetheless, I still had hopes of making the varsity team during my senior year. As our JV season came to an end, I had to develop a strategy to make the team so I chose to become the best 3-point shooter I could possibly be. This decision was based on the fact that the recent year's varsity team built its entire offense around the jump-shooting ability of Jono Metzger-Jones. He was the best shooter in the Bay Area at the time, so I figured that was what I would become.

Between the end of the JV season and varsity tryouts, I dedicated myself to going to the YMCA every Saturday and making 1,000 jump shots. There is a stark difference between making 1,000 shots and shooting 1,000 shots. I could make about 100 shots every 30 minutes, so I spent the first six hours of my Saturday shooting. Only after reaching my goal of 1,000 would I start playing in pick-up games. On

LIL WAYNE & JAY-Z COMPARISON

	LIL WAYNE	JAY-Z
Real Name	Dwayne Carter	Sean Carter
Birth date	September 27, 1982 (27)	December 4, 1969 (39)
Alter ego	Weezy F. Baby	Young Hova
Record Label	Young Money Records	Roc-a-fella Records
Presidents of...	Cash Money Records	Def Jam Records
Role Models	2Pac, Jay-Z	Notorious B.I.G., Jaz O
Neighborhood	Hollygrove, LA	Marcy, NY
Years in the Rapping	10 years	13 years
First Solo Album	*Tha Block Is Hot*, 1999 (17)	*Reasonable Doubt*, 1996 (27)
Album Series	*Tha Carter, Tha Carter II, Tha Carter III*	*In My Lifetime, Volume 1, Hard Knock Life, Volume 2, Life & Times of S. Carter, Volume 3*
Number of Songs	500+	400+
Grammy Nominations	8	30
Grammy Wins	3	7
Total Solo Albums	6	10

Sunday and Monday, my shooting shoulder was sore, but my muscle memory was strengthening. When scrimmages began for the varsity team for anyone considering trying out, my jump shot was on target. Though I probably became the best 3-point shooter in the Bay Area for that given period, there are other aspects of being a great basketball player that I didn't have. In the end, I didn't make the team, however, I know that I achieved my personal best.

I've only committed to being my best at three things over the course of my entire life: the best high school 3-point shooter in the Bay Area, the best Calculus student in high school, and the best purposefinder I can be. Each of these required a practice routine that was above and beyond what my teammates, classmates, and colleagues were willing to do. Though I got cut from the varsity basketball team and got a C in calculus during my freshman year at UCLA, I know that I reached my personal best despite the outcome. Hopefully, I can use those lessons in excellence to fair better as a purposefinder.

As I seek to become the world leader in helping individuals and organizations align their lives with their purpose through group experience creation, motivational teaching and speaking, and writing, I refer back to these moments in high school for inspiration. Between high school graduation in June of 2000 and the moment I quit my job in January of 2009, I was always *good enough*. I was *good enough* to graduate from UCLA with a 3.3 GPA in three years, get a high-responsibility job directing a non-profit straight out of college, and get into one of the world's top MBA programs at Stanford at the age 23. Despite being *good enough* to achieve many things over the past nine years, my decision to become a purposefinder is my first conscious commitment to pursue long-term *greatness*. Most people settle for good enough and end up average. If you ask people what they are currently committed to being their best at doing, most people won't have an answer.

POSITIONING AS LANE

Positioning is the lane in life where your personal velocity is the highest and where you're willing to be a pioneer and lead. In physics, velocity is defined as distance over time (i.e. car speed is measured in miles per hour). Your velocities vary based on the different types of roads you choose to take, so the quest is to find the road where your personal velocity is at its highest. A Hummer won't beat a Ferrari on an open road, but it will beat a Ferrari on a safari. **Like these specialty cars, you are specifically built for a particular path that matches your build in character and skills and you must find the key to succeeding based on the route you've chosen.**

In the same way that we pay a premium for airplanes, trains, and cars according to the velocities in which they can condense physical spaces for passengers, other people (such as customers, clients) and organizations (like employers) will pay you for getting them from point A (where they are) to point B (where they want to go) financially, organizationally, spiritually, mentally, etc. If you are able to powerfully close space between two events for yourself, another person, or another entity, you will create value, which you can store for later use as money. Airplanes use the sky. Trains use tracks. Cars use roads. **Therefore, in order for you to create and capture the most value you can and get rich (spiritually, financially, etc.), you must become aware of where your personal velocity is the**

highest and stay in that lane.

Identifying the lane where your personal and professional velocity is at its highest isn't always straightforward. The best ways to discover your lane include listening for what people you work with say you're great at, asking friends what they think you would be great at if you weren't in your existing job, and exposing yourself to as many lanes as possible. Awareness of what you're great at doing will allow you to be **ex-speed-ient (quickly capitalizing on purposeful opportunities)** in your personal and professional life. Once you identify the avenues where your personal velocity is at its highest, you can align with professional opportunities, projects, and employers that will allow you to perform most powerfully. **You will only be in the express lane of life once you're fully expressed, for your purpose is the highest form of self-expression there is.**

One of the most difficult aspects of the career search is identifying the professional lane, industry, or role where your unique combination of skills and experiences will allow you to achieve our highest personal and professional velocity. One of the greatest examples of the difference between someone in the right lane and the wrong lane is Michael Jordan's story. After establishing himself as the world's best basketball player and leading the Chicago Bulls to three NBA championships, Jordan retired from professional basketball. Less than a year later, Jordan signed a minor league baseball contract to fulfill the dreams of his late father who envisioned his son playing professional baseball, not basketball. Despite requiring some similar mental and physical skill sets, such as quick thinking, positioning, speed, and hand-eye coordination, Jordan's athleticism did not produce similar results on the baseball field. Realizing the misalignment, Jordan returned to the NBA a year later and led the Chicago Bulls to three more championships before retiring again, coming back, and retiring a third time. In 2009, Michael Jordan was inducted into The Naismith Memorial Basketball Hall of Fame.

Seth Godin, one of the world's leading marketing experts, calls this hiatus, "the dip." In his book *The Dip*, he explains the effort and return curve. Most people think that there is a linear relationship between effort and return, meaning that the more effort they put into what they are doing, the more return they will get. Godin argues that after some beginner's luck at the start, there is actually a dip where people or companies who aren't truly passionate about being the best at what they do quit while those who are truly passionate work through the dip. This dip essentially weeds out the real from the fake. The dip also suggests that you need to quit anything that you're not willing to be your best at professionally and that before starting anything, you should ask yourself if you are willing to work through the dip.

In terms of mastery, I've noticed that people who learn how to master one thing first have an easier time mastering others. People who master one language have easier time learning a second, third, fourth, and fifth. The same goes for learning instruments. Once you understand the process of mastery, you can apply it to any subject, field, industry, or lane that you want. Though we're taught in school to be good at everything and well-rounded, the people who succeed in life get great at one thing and then selectively choose opportunities that will allow them to exhibit their greatness against well-rounded people.

There is a false perception in the world that the most common route is always the shortest route when considering distance and time. The most common route isn't the best route for everyone. Some people like the scenic route. Some people like the fastest route. On Google Maps, there is even an option to get directions that avoid highways for people who like taking the side-streets. The route you take depends heavily on what matters to you most. While someone who is late, in a rush, or thinks time is scarce may take what they think is the fastest route, someone else who is more patient and enjoys time as it passes may be open to taking the scenic route. Instead of comparing your speed or your route to everyone else's, you should simply find the route that aligns with your values and be fully content whether people are seemingly passing you or appearing to enjoy their route more than you are enjoying your own. Fear of feeling behind can cause you to make decisions that are not in a-line-meant with your purpose and take you off your course. By traveling the route that is best for you, you will have *in-sights* **(glimpses of the greatness within yourself)**, while others just get *excited* from seeing sites.

Positioning also has to do with your desired pace. Most speedometers go up to 150 mph, but in most states the speed limit is below 70 mph. Just because the car goes that fast doesn't mean that you have to drive that fast. Your highest personal velocity is for moments of flow when peak performance is required. Like our cars, our minds and bodies are equipped to do amazing things, but we must identify the lane and pace that is best for us on this particular stretch of the journey of life.

Positioning is the skill or subject you consciously declare that you want to be your best at based on your strengths and passions. Your strengths are the things you do well that make you feel stronger, however strengths atrophy unless you dedicate time and energy to practicing them. In his book *Soar With Your Strengths*, Don Clifton, a lead researcher for the Gallup organization and pioneer of the strength-based revolution, defines strengths as "a pattern of behavior, thoughts, and feelings that produces a high degree of satisfaction and pride; generates both psychic and/or financial reward; and presents measurable progress toward excellence." Strengths can be discovered through your yearnings, satisfaction, areas of rapid learning, and where we experience flow. According to the book, Clifton's journey began with the simple creative quest-ion, "What would happen if we studied what was right with people versus what's wrong with people?" Clifton's work has inspired over 50 years of research of thousands of successful people and has been repurposed in the Gallup *StrengthsFinder 2.0* book and online questionnaire to help anyone discover their top five strengths in 30 minutes so that they can focus on their few strengths and achieve greatness rather than give their energy to all of their weaknesses and ending up average.

Our attempt to create well-rounded people, assumes we can be great at everything, but that is impossible if greatness requires practice and time is limited. **Jacks-of-all-trades are usually average at all trades, yet our education system and corporate infrastructures still encourage trying to know it all.** Especially in today's job market, companies want you to know how to do everything, when that actually limits the potential for greatness in you and them. **The ideal team has great individuals in the right position as opposed to having a group of people who are average at everything.** As information becomes more accessible and expands as a result of the internet, it will become increasingly difficult for anyone to master multiple areas at once.

Your positioning is your declaration to become so great at something that your weaknesses pale in comparison to your strengths. For example, four-time NBA champion Shaquille O'Neil's strength and ability to score in the low post make his poor free-throw shooting almost irrelevant. Clifton's work in strength-finding encourages individuals and society to work together to organize a world where everyone is in their proper position, meaning that they are using their strengths as much as possible. Tom Rath and Marcus Buckingham, authors of *StrengthsFinder 2.0* and *Go Put Your Strengths To Work*, now champion Clifton's work.

The combination of your principles, passions, problems, and people uniquely position you to master some skill or subject matter. Dependent on the complexity of the skill or subject, it may take a lifetime to master it but 10,000 hours of focused practice will definitely set you apart. Pioneer means being the first to do something, but positioning means commitment to being your best. **It is possible to be first without being your best and it is possible to be your best without being first.**

Your very own pioneers are leaders in your eyes for some reason and now it is time to identify what you want to pioneer. As a path-specific pioneer, you may want to be a lead thinker on a particular subject or you may want to be the best at a particular skill. After losing the presidency in 2000 to George Bush, Al Gore chose to become the lead voice on global warming. His film, *An Inconvenient Truth*, was the manifestation of years of study from his pioneers before he eventually became the face of the movement.

Gore's ability to channel the same energy he used to try to win the 2000 United States presidential election has allowed him to become the lead thinker on global warming only a few years later.

Positioning is not about being #1 in the world or a competition. It is a commitment to being the best version of YOU that you can be and being YOUR best at whatever it is you choose to do. Therefore, positioning is not a competition for first place against someone else. Positioning is a competition between "who you are" versus "who you want to be" and a competition between "where you are" versus "where you want to be". The key to great positioning is first to align who you are and who you want to be. When these two are aligned, you are living an authentic life. The next step is to align where you are with where you want to go. This is personal achievement. People unclear on where they want to go, end up traveling incredible distances in life but feel unaccomplished. Aimless driving is a waste of time and energy. **Your first goal should be to be authentic, for achievement without authenticity is hard to sustain because it requires living a constant lie.**

The *Guinness Book of World Records* cites people who chose to be the best in the world at something—whether it's hot dog-eating king Joey Chestnut devouring 60 hot dogs in 12 minutes or Marek Turowski creating the world's fastest furniture with his motorized sofa. **Very few people end up in the *Guinness Book of World Records* by luck or by biology**. **Becoming the best at anything is a conscious choice, not a birthright**. In addition, many people have made a living off of that one thing they are recognized for no matter how obscure. Joey Chestnut won $10,000 for placing first in Nathan's hot dog-eating contest. That's $167 per hot dog eaten or $82 per minute. When you're the best at something and people know you're the best at it, money will come.

We each have at least two opportunities to be in the *Guinness Book of World Records*: one, for being ourselves, and two, for the manifestations of being ourselves. The difference between the two is subtle, but substantial. The prerequisite of sustainable success is authenticity—meaning that someone is true to themselves at all times. Though being a great you is rarely rewarded in a celebrity-driven society that teaches us to emulate others, being a great you sets the stage for the manifestations of a great you, which is what we tend to award people for. The difference between being ourselves and the manifestations of being ourselves is the difference between someone who is awarded a lifetime achievement award versus someone who is awarded a one-time achievement award. Lifetime achievement awards are given for long-term consistency and commitment and usually come along with many one-time awards, which are the manifestations of a person's being. **Unfortunately, *in-the-moment* awards are more common than *every-moment* awards. For every lifetime achievement award given, there are hundreds of one-time achievement awards given.** By simply being ourselves, great things naturally happen often. Greatness only comes by luck when you aren't your authentic self.

PERSONAL POSITIONING

Almost all vehicles have names that suit their style. My first car out of college was a Ford Mustang. A mustang is a free-roaming wild horse of the North American West. Similar to the horse, the car represented youthful wildness and freedom and was manufactured in North America. Other fitting vehicle names that speak to their purpose are the Nissan Pathfinder, the Subaru Outback, the Honda Civic, and the Toyota Land Cruiser. Though people don't buy vehicles according to their names, when a product or service is properly named, the people who need and value it most can find it more easily.

When it comes to naming people in some indigenous cultures, names were given according to your purpose as well. In some practices, people underwent multiple naming ceremonies at birth, during adolescence and then adulthood based on their accomplishments, characteristics, and responsibilities. For instance, Sitting Bull, one of the most well-known Sioux Indians was born with the name Jumping Badger because of his speed. He was later given the name Jumping Bull as a young adult, and then became Sitting Bull because he slow, yet great decision-making, before taking action.

Sometimes our nicknames are more telling of who we are than our given names. Without a naming ceremony, parents tend to choose names that sound cute. Most names have some sort of meaning or legacy, and sometimes our lives parallel those who have bore the name before us. For instance, I don't think it is a coincidence that Juliette Gordon founded the Girl Scouts, which is very similar to the movement I am creating for millennials almost 100 years later. Nicknames usually come from the conscious choice of someone close to us. At any given moment, they choose to forgo using our given name and call us something different because they feel it is a more accurate depiction of who we truly are. Some of my nicknames include Navigator Newt (for my sense of direction), J-Love (for my loving nature), J-

Conxus (for my consciousness), and J-Money (for my business acumen).

Nicknames are just the beginning. They communicate back to us what we've communicated to others through the way we live. But even more powerful than accepting a nickname is choosing your own superhero name. Your superhero name should communicate your uniqueness and how you create value for the other people. Some good ones on TV are The Dog Whisper, a guy who has the power to train dogs, and The Locator, a guy who helps people track down lost family members. Good places to look for your superhero name are your e-mail addresses, screen names, and passwords. In the Department of Motivated Vehicles community, we only call each other by our superhero names because they speak to our purpose and essence. **Your superhero name is the name of your main life vehicle in the same way that the Nissan Pathfinder describes its off-road 4x4 vehicle. You are the driver of that vehicle.** You may have other vehicles or roles in the garage of your life, but your main vehicle should reflect the superhero in you.

If I am going to become the best purposefinder that I can be, I have to become great at what people expect a great purposefinder to do. Through talking to people, I have discovered that the two skills vital to my success are motivational speaking and writing. Oral communication is essential to being my best so I pursue and accept any opportunity I can to speak in front of people. I've reached approximately 5,000 people through my keynote speeches, presentations, and YouTube videos. To practice daily, I bought voice-to-text software so that that I can practice my speaking and writing at the same time. I also use the shower

SUPERHERO NAMES FROM DRIVING SCHOOL FOR LIFE

The Advocate	The Enlightener	Pain Buster
Big Change	The Explorer	Potential Pusher
bReignStorm	The Gatekeeper	The Prophet
Bridge Builder	Ghetto Man the Prophet	Rebel Entrepreneur
CEO	Ghost Speaker	Reflector
Charlie the Great	Heavenly Glory	Sharp Shooter
The Clenched Fist	The Justice	Show Time
Coach	Justin-Time	Storyteller
The Connector	The Innovator	The Sythesizer
The Conscious Hustla	The Life Guard	The Third-Eye Transformer
The Chancellor	The Life Changer	Truth Bearer
Correspondence	The Materialist	Truth Seeker
The Creator	The Mayor	Poetic Soul
Deus Style	Melody Moses	Poverty Killer
Mr. Miracle	The Mirror	Voice of the Go Getter
Dr. Grow	The Music Making Do	The Warden
Dream Catcher	Gooder	Wellness Guru
Elevator	The Negotiator	

to do motivational speeches while a lot of people use it to sing. Through blogging (at www.julliengordon.com) and tweeting (@PurposeFinder) I sharpen my ability to articulate my thoughts, connect with my audience, and write books like this one. I have reached over 100,000 people through my blog. When I observe some of my path-specific pioneers like Michael Beckwith, Eckhart Tolle, Rick Warren, Tony Robbins, and Deepak Chopra, they are all amazing oral and written communicators.

PROFESSIONAL LANES

Professional positioning is really about self-branding within your company, community, and beyond. So this begs the question, "Beyond your job or leadership title, what are you known for in your company or community?" Are you the Deal Closer? The Negotiator? The Chief Cultivator? The Lead

Generator? The Relationship Builder? The Marketing Guy? The Penny Saver? The Innovator? The Deliverer? **The more well-known you are in a company or a community based on the value you're creating, the more security you have in that space. Who is going to fire The Deal Closer?** Any given team will have multiple project managers, sales representatives, or customer service agents, but your superhero name captures the unique value you're creating for your company or community beyond your job title and description. Your job description says one thing but the script you write with your daily performance can say another.

In the chapter on passions, we discussed finding your passion, but positioning is about excelling at your passions. The greatest challenge in crystallizing a passion into a valuable skill is developing a practice plan and disciplining oneself to stick to it. That's where coaches and mentors come in. If you want to be a better businessman or businesswoman it's obvious that you should you do more business, but that's like saying a basketball player should simply play more basketball. It's not specific enough. Though both statements are true, we have to find a more concrete way to articulate how one becomes better at doing what they want to be great at by identifying a vital combination of skills for greatness and figuring out how to practice them regularly. Coaches and mentors can help you develop the right practice plan for your desired position.

There is a clear distinction between someone who practices and some who just plays. In order for your passions to crystallize into valuable skills, we have to practice, practice, and practice until the difference between you and an amateur is evident. The difference between someone who has crystallized their passion into a skill and someone who

COMPANY PROFILE:
POSITIONING & SOUTHWEST AIRLINES

Southwest Airlines has successfully positioned itself as the low-cost provider in airlines. Based on an interview with Founder & CEO Herb Khellher, Jerry Porras writes in *Success Built To Last* that, "What hit him so unexpectedly was a populist passion to cure a perceived injustice—it was simply too expensive for a majority of Americans to fly." Herb Khellher's focus on low cost flew Southwest Airlines to 69 profitable quarters in an industry ridden with bankruptcy while also providing the lowest costs across the country.

Despite increasing expenses, Southwest Airlines stays dedicated to their promise. If you go to their website, they have an entire page dedicated to how they save the customer on price. While other airlines have fees for checking bags, changing flights, window and aisle seats, and snacks, Southwest offers all of those things for free and still provides the lowest price. They have kept costs low for their customers through their amazing company culture that attracts talent at below-market rates, their ability to get the most out of planes by keeping them in the air, their reliance on the Boeing 737 as their only type of plane, and their fuel-hedging program to mitigate fluctuations in the price of fuel.

Even with their first two unprofitable quarters in the second half of 2009 and the entrance of new airlines like Jet Blue and Song, Southwest is still positioned as the lowest-cost carrier in the country. For the past 37 years, Southwest has held fast to its mission of "dedication to the highest quality of Customer Service delivered with a sense of warmth, friendliness, individual pride, and Company Spirit." Their care for their employees translates into care for their customers and feeling LUV (their stock market ticker) is more valuable than having a TV, wider seat, or priority boarding on a plane.

hasn't is in their ability to replicate success. **An uncrystallized passion shines randomly whereas a crystallized passion shines when it wants or needs to.**

Through Steve Pavlina's blog, I discovered Charlie Cook's "15 Second Marketing" technique. The key takeaway is that you should communicate who you are according to the value you add for people and organizations rather than your name or title. Whenever you meet someone new, the dreaded question always arises. "So what do you do?"

Most people answer like this:

"I'm a marketing director at a top-tier advertising agency. I develop strategies and messages that will appeal to future customers."

And the conversation ends there because people assume that they know the entirety of what you do based on their limited understanding of marketing, therefore, they don't ask any more questions or they just aren't interested in it (usually because you aren't interested in it either). But, imagine answering like this:

"They call me the Cupid. I help companies identify customers who will fall in love with their products and then help them develop strategies and messaging to pierce them in the heart." By answering with your superhero name and super power, you spark curiosity because this will likely be the first time anyone has heard an answer like this. By using the word "they" you are suggesting that you have external validation. Finally, by stating how you help people rather than running off your weekly to-do list, the person can decipher the value you add to the world and potentially themselves.

MODERN DAY SUPERHEROES

GIVEN NAME	SUPERHERO NAME	SUPER POWER
Cesar Milan	Dog Whisperer	The power to connect with dogs and train them to behave
Troy Dunn	The Locator	The power to help people locate long lost family members
Oscar Pistorius	Blade Runner	The power to run extremely fast with prosthetic legs
Steve Irwin	The Crocodile Hunter	The power to tame crocodiles and other animals
Stephen Wiltshire	The Human Camera	The power to capture complex image in his head (i.e. the entire birds-eye view of a city) and then draw it from memory despite having autism.

In business, positioning is a term companies use to describe how they want to look to customers in comparison to competitors. If the company has a unique ability to produce or acquire things at low prices due to its scale, then it may position itself as the low-price leader. In order to create the most value for your company, you need to know how your role within the organization solidifies its positioning and affects the bottom line. For example, as the Chief Technology Officer of Super Mart, I leverage technology to increase the flow of data to and from stores so that employees and managers can make accurate decisions in regards to inventory thus:

- Keeping all shelves stocked so that customers can always find what they want which increases sales
- Shaping purchasing decisions based on inventory

turns so that we can capitalize on volume discounts while never buying more than we can sell, and
- Reducing spoilage of fresh foods and the extra costs associated with waste

When you, your team, and your company are clear on how you're creating value on a daily basis, it's hard to get fired. **Average people get fired—exceptional people don't.**

EXPANDING CAREER OPTIONS

There are millions of career paths out there, but growing up, we are often limited to doctor, lawyer, teacher, businessperson, and engineer because those are the five professional degrees on which institutions of higher education focus. In addition, some of the most popular TV series like *Law & Order, ER, Scrubs,* and *Boston Public* keep these professional paths at the forefront of our minds. But what about the people who don't travel those routes? What do they do for a living?

In the Driving School for Life course, there is a quick ice-breaker that challenges participants to come with a career for each letter of the alphabet. At first it seems easy— architect, banker, chef. But after a while, people start to slow down drastically. I know that some letters have less career paths associated with them than others, but the point of the exercise is show how limited our thinking is about the number of career paths out there. **How can you choose appropriately if you haven't even explored all of your options?** When everyone shares their answers, there are usually very few duplicates and collectively we have over 500 career paths available. I guarantee that 1. Someone is getting paid to do everything listed and 2. If you are the top

10 in the world at any of those paths, no matter how obscure (i.e. zebra stripe counter), you will be satisfied with the financial compensation. To do the exercise, turn to the end of the chapter and set a timer for five minutes and see how far you get.

We also get caught up in brand names and wanting to work for companies that people recognize instead of companies that will give you the opportunity to recognize your full potential. Have you ever been driving down the freeway and wondered what all of those no-brand name companies do? Who works in that building? You will see that opportunities are all around you if you just open your mind and expand your options. The next time you pass a commercial building with a company name you don't recognize, write it down and explore it on the Internet as an exercise to expand your map of career possibilities.

CONCLUSION

Society encourages us to diversify instead of specialize and as a result we become the jacks-of-all-trades and masters of none. The same people that say "don't put all of your eggs in one basket" are usually the same ones with one egg in too many baskets. In the financial markets, people who hedge their bets end up with average performance, whereas people who take educated risks either win big or lose small. Education has always driven us to diversify our knowledge base even though excellence requires specialization initially. Very few college majors track perfectly into a career path. In fact, the people who make a difference develop deep knowledge in one area that they are able to apply to many areas thereafter. Similarly, learning one language or musical instrument well makes it easier to pick up new languages and instruments later on.

Happiness is relative. Therefore, though average material wealth has increased dramatically in comparison to previous generations, nobody feels like they have more than they had before. As a result, very few people are actually happier and more fulfilled emotionally despite significant material increase. The fulfillment of purpose is different than financial profits or material gain. The pursuit of purpose is limited by time, not money. **People are fully aware of their bank account balances but nobody knows what's in their time account.** The earlier you put a stake in the ground, the more time you'll have to reach your 10,000 hours of practice and enjoy your journey toward expertise. By accepting the challenge of mastery and greatness, the tangible results from your focused energy on skills and subjects that are meaningful to you will come with time.

Your positioning becomes your brand. It's the words that immediately come to mind when people think about you based on a skill or subject you've mastered. When I think of Al Gore, I think global warming. Bill Gates equals computers. Google equals search. In small rural communities, roles become just as pervasive as names. Roles could include: farmer, teacher, minister, or grocer. Community members were clear on who had what skill set and therefore knew who to approach when the need arose for a particular expertise. I self-identify as a purposefinder. That is what I believe my role in the world is and I vow to practice to be the best purposefinder I can be. If I am successful at what I do, when you feel lost or stuck and need motivation or direction, you will think of me. What problems or situations will trigger people to think about you and the value you have to offer personally and professionally?

A-Z CAREER PATHS

Directions: Write down a potential career path for each letter of the alphabet. Be as original and innovative as possible. You have 5 minutes.

A		**N**	
B		**O**	
C		**P**	
D		**Q**	
E		**R**	
F		**S**	
G		**T**	
H		**U**	
I		**V**	
J		**W**	
K		**X**	
L		**Y**	
M		**Z**	

CONCRETE PLANS
& ROUTE-TINES

Directions: Create a super hero name for yourself and define what you want to be the world's best at doing. List 3 super powers, skills, strengths, or abilities connected to your name and positioning. Come up with two **route-ines (a set of daily, weekly, or monthly actions to maintain progress)**. Your superhero should be consistent in your personal and professional life.

Example Power: Ability to inspire people instantaneously

Route-ine E.1: Create conversations about life with 2 or more people weekly

Route-ine E.2: Read inspirational quotes, blogs, or books every day

Super Hero Name: ....

I'm committed to being the best in the world at:...............

....

Power #1:..

Route-ine 1.1:..
I will do this .... times/day or .... times/week, which equals .... hr/week

Route-ine 1.2:...

I will do this .... times/day or .... times/week, which equals .... hr/week

Power #2:...

Route-ine 2.1:...

I will do this .... times/day or .... times/week, which equals .... hr/week

Route-ine 2.2:...

I will do this .... times/day or .... times/week, which equals .... hr/week

Power #3:...

Route-ine 3.1:...

I will do this .... times/day or .... times/week, which equals .... hr/week

Route-ine 3.2:...

I will do this .... times/day or .... times/week, which equals .... hr/week

MOVE-MEANT

Where The Rubber Meets The Road

Below are specific actions you can do in the next 30 days to align your life a little bit more with your personal and professional positioning.

Personal: Send an email out to your friends, family, and advisors asking them 1. What they think you have the potential to be great at if your current career path were to disappear? and 2. When have they seen you exhibit greatness in their lives?

Professional: Ask a few trusted mentors or colleagues what they would expect from someone who said they were the best in the world at...................................... (put your positioning here). Aggregate their answers to create your criteria for greatness.

YOU CAN BE
YOUR BEST
WITHOUT
BEING THE

BEST

AND YOU CAN BE THE BEST
WITHOUT BEING YOUR BEST

PIONEERS »
YOUR PACE CARS

THE PURPOSE OF THIS CHAPTER IS TO:

- Identify the characteristics of great personal and professional pioneers
- Define three ways for you to follow your pioneers

GUIDING QUEST-IONS:

Personal: Who are my models, mentors, and guides?

Professional: Who are the old and new industry leaders? How is my professional position helping us be an industry leader?

QUOTES:

"Do not go where the path may lead; go instead where there is no path and leave a trail."
— Ralph Waldo Emerson

"The best way to predict the future is to create it."
— Divine Bradley

OPRAH WINFREY'S PIONEER: PHIL DONAHUE

In a 1988 article in the *New York Times*, Oprah Winfrey spoke on the importance of Phil Donahue and his show to her path. "If there never had been a Phil, there never would have been a me. I can talk about things now that I never could have talked about before he came on the air. There's room for both of us." There wasn't enough room. The 42-year-old Winfrey surpassed her pioneer Phil Donahue in ratings, publicity, and acclaim after competing for 12 years in the same time slot. In May of 1996, Donahue aired his last episode, passing the baton to Winfrey to lead the talk show industry with her affectionate personality. Her style allowed her to reach her audience in ways that Donahue couldn't, as well as create new audiences as she shifted the direction of the industry with her topics, style, and guests.

The media built up their head-to-head competition as if it were a presidential election. That wasn't the case. Phil Donahue began in 1967. By that time, the concept of talk shows was only 20 years old with its origins in radio. As televisions filled households nationwide, talk shows became more popular. Talk shows were an opportunity for viewers to vicariously connect with celebrities of whom they were fans. Donahue rode the paths paved by Dave Garroway, Merv Griffin, and Mike Douglas. However, his content was focused on divisive issues that agitated his audience into active participation. Donahue was known for running up and down aisles with his wireless microphone. Even with his mic and controversial topics, Winfrey's shift into his lane struck a chord with women and they caravanned over to her.

Winfrey brought a new style to talk shows that had never been seen before. First and foremost, she was an African-

American woman in a space dominated by white men. *Time* magazine wrote:

"Few people would have bet on Oprah Winfrey's swift rise to host of the most popular talk show on TV. In a field dominated by white males, she is a black female of ample bulk. As interviewers go, she is no match for, say, Phil Donahue...What she lacks in journalistic toughness, she makes up for in plainspoken curiosity, robust humor and, above all empathy. Guests with sad stories to tell are apt to rouse a tear in Oprah's eye...They, in turn, often find themselves revealing things they would not imagine telling anyone, much less a national TV audience. It is the talk show as a group therapy session."

Winfrey was helping people—sometimes by even using herself as an example—transform their lives by merging personal development, spirituality, and health into 60 minutes. Her authenticity and energy captured the hearts of her audience and has allowed her and other female talk show hosts to flourish.

MY PIONEER: DR. EDWARD "CHIP" ANDERSON

Three days into my first quarter at UCLA, I couldn't get all of the classes I needed for my major so I needed a schedule-filler to increase my units. I just looked for classes based on their time rather than their content. I came across an interesting class titled "EDUC92F: Academic Success in the Undergraduate Experience." Bruce Barbee and Chip Anderson taught it on two mornings that aligned perfectly with my schedule. Chip had a personable and practical teaching style that I had only experienced twice before in my academic career. I could tell he genuinely cared about our personal growth as well as our academic achievement.

Chip believed in strengths-based learning and living. He co-authored *StrengthsQuest: Discover and Develop Your Strengths in Academics, Career, and Beyond* with Don Clifton of the Gallup Organization. The book and test was designed to help people identify their top 5 strengths and use them in their everyday lives. I believed in the strengths-based revolution and met with Chip every morning he was on campus for nearly three years. He and I got to know each very well over that time. Like my mother, he dealt with alcoholism in his lifetime, but it was cancer that would later take his life. Interestingly enough, Chip and I had the exact same top 5 strengths: belief, strategic, activator, achiever, and connectedness. His impact on my life and the lives of others is best described in his own words about his strengths:

"I have Belief, Strategic, Activator, Achiever and Connectedness as my Signature Themes. My visual image of how my talents in these themes work together is of a rocket standing upright on a launch pad. My Belief talents form a giant foundational launch pad. The meaning, purpose and direction stemming from my core beliefs generate a tremendous amount of power that enables me to impact people. The fuselage of my rocket stands upright on the middle of the launch pad. This is my Activator theme that enables me to turn ideas into actions that generate revolutionary changes. On each side of the fuselage are two booster rockets. One I call Strategic and the other Achiever. The Strategic helps me see multiple alternatives to reaching a goal, and the Achiever means I am in constant motion to reach my goals—I have daily goals on pieces of paper stuck in my shirt pocket that keep me focused on what God wants

me to do that day, but I also have ultimate goals, and those are always tied to excellence—to being the person God wants me to be. The nose cone on top of the main fuselage is Connectedness. With Connectedness, I realize there is a 'Master plan' that brings each person into my life, and I know that what I do with my life will have a "ripple effect" long after I am gone."

He advocated for a strengths-based revolution in education, where students were taught to focus on developing their strengths as opposed to fixing their weaknesses. After he passed away from cancer in 2005, I committed myself to taking his revolution one step further by creating a tool that could help people gain clarity on their life purpose, hence my superhero name, Purposefinder. Alone, strengths are neutral and can be used for good or bad, but I believe that if one knows their strengths and their purpose, they are a more powerful being in the world than a person who just knows their strengths. The 8 Cylinders of Success is my attempt to build upon the momentum Chip created with his life.

PIONEERS AS PACE CAR

On the journey of life, we all drive under the influence, however, in this case I don't mean alcohol. Our pioneers have influenced us all. Pioneers are the cars ahead of you that have set the tempo and paved the way for you thus far, but will either one day off-ramp or be overtaken by you as you progress on your journey. As you follow, you should observe closely and learn from their successes and mistakes. Their brake lights and their speed are signals that can guide your personal journey. You should get close—but not too close—while still ensuring that you don't lose your ability to think independently in an attempt to carbon copy the path they have carved for themselves. **Ten-car pile-ups only occur when multiple people are following each other blindly or too closely.**

Inherently, pioneers aren't followers, but they've typically followed someone else before branching out on their own unique paths. Since we each have a unique destine-nation, pioneers can only guide us to a certain extent. There will be crossroads in your life where you choose to go separate ways than your pioneers. At that time, you may find a new pioneer or start paving a path of your own. Ultimately, the value of a pioneer is in their experience driving amidst uncertainty more so than their ability to explain exactly how to get to where they've been. **You want to follow someone who can *navigate the unexpected* rather than someone who just *expects to navigate*. You should only follow pioneers to learn from them, not to become them.**

Pioneers are people who are the first to travel into uncharted territory. We all have the potential to be pioneers if we remain independent thinkers. Independent thoughts are the seeds of creation. When you are charting new territory, there is no map. Pioneers may discover new terrain within a pre-existing lane or they may create an entirely new lane of thought altogether based on their picture of the world. **While most people just see a map on a table, pioneers consider the entire room, the map, and the table. And in that *room* is plenty of *room for error* since pioneers try things that have never been done before.** Pioneers go where no one else has gone and have visions to go even further.

Thus, pioneers are potential models, mentors, examples, and guides who have courageously stepped off the map.

Though the things that pioneers discover and accomplish are inspiring, we should also honor pioneers for their courage. How they think and view the world is more important than what they do or accomplish. Therefore, a pioneer doesn't have to be someone who is doing exactly what you want to do. **A pioneer can be anyone whose principles cause you to think beyond where you originally planned to go with your life and ideas.**

The hope of any true pioneer is for another person to go even further than they went. To stop where they leave off is like standing still with the baton of progress. Standing with the baton is worse than attempting to run and dropping it. At least dropping it means that you tried to go forward and simply made a mistake. **Mistakes and experimentation are commonplace on the journey of a pioneer because there are no definitive right answers amidst uncertainty and information that is far from perfect.** Initially most pioneers are rejected. Nonetheless, pioneers uphold their principles even when the rest of the world erroneously rejects them because of their beliefs. This is the same belief we must feed off of as we transition from followers to leaders to pioneers. It's only after deeming most of our greatest pioneers crazy for a majority of their lives that we end up glorifying them as the maps they paved with their lives eventually start to materialize in the minds of the masses.

WHERE TO FIND PIONEERS

As stated before, a pioneer doesn't have to be someone who is doing exactly what you want to do or be a celebrity. A pioneer is someone who embodies characteristics you admire and upholds their personal principles in the face of opposition or uncertainty because they believe there is **an**

alter-native (a new way that differs from the status quo) way beyond the existing map of possibilities. Many of us are only comfortable with our native land of thought, whereas pioneers train for new terrain. Alter-natives that extend beyond what comes natural to you are always possible even if they aren't visible.

Pioneers can include managers, colleagues, parents, peers, community leaders, teachers, ministers, historical figures, or organizations. Choosing pioneers is more about observing one's state of being rather than admiring their accomplishments. We should be more concerned with how one travels through life than how far they traveled or what they accomplished since both of these outcomes are a result of their state of being and how they travel.

From my experience, people's pioneers are more likely to be people that they have personal relationships with rather than celebrities that everyone knows. The ideal situation is to find a mentor that you deem to be a pioneer in your lane, however, keep in mind that mentors aren't inherently pioneers. Our close connections to these people over time allow us to observe them in good and bad times. Regardless of circumstances, we find that these peoples' characters do not change. **They are who they are no matter how they are or where they are.** Pioneers tend to have an optimistic view of life and they give us new ideas, hope, and inspiration. They also have a knack for teaching without preaching by sharing their experiences and then giving you the freedom to choose your path. **Their ultimate goal isn't to replicate themselves; their goal is to help you be the best you, whoever that may be. Through their self-leadership, they eventually create more pioneers.**

There are also path-specific pioneers, which often refer to industry thought-leaders. The difference between a thought-leader and an industry-leader is that thought-leaders push the industry forward and see what is possible in the near future. Industry-leaders on the other hand may only be leading because they were pioneers of the past. Sometimes success causes industry-leaders and individuals to stop innovating when in fact, their innovation is what got them where they are today. We have to keep thinking like pioneers, even and especially, if we're in front.

Whether dead or alive, pioneers of the past and the present can serve as great guides for us on our journeys. Biographies and autobiographies are a great way to travel back in time and step inside the lives of pioneers you respect. There are very few biographies and autobiographies written about people who lived average lives. Following your pioneers means studying their mindset and understanding where the lane was when they inherited it and where they extended it to with their life so that you can contemplate how you will take what they accomplished even further.

PERSONAL PACE CARS

We must all ask ourselves "What am I disrupting with my life?" Interrupting the current conversation in the world is a prerequisite for all pioneers. Interruption is rude when it stops the conversation, however it leads to new thought when its intention is to advance the conversation. As a pioneer, you must be in-true-sive with your beliefs in a world that tells you to always be polite and politically correct. **In-true-sive means to speak your truth within you without fear of judgment or conflict, especially when the prevailing truth—even if widely**

accepted—feels wrong to you. Though we live in a democratic society where majority rules, the majority aren't always right.

If the shoe fits, then it probably isn't big enough. We need shoes that we can grow into and visions that expand beyond what we already know is possible. The purpose of a pioneer is not for you to fit in their shoes and replicate what they did and where they went. Pioneers don't walk in someone else's shoes or shadow forever. No one has walked your path before, so you have the opportunity to be a pioneer if you accept it. Since everyone's path is unique, the road is also narrow. And the narrow road will not be concrete until you pave it with your own two feet. We want the concrete to already be there so that we can be certain of our next step, but you can't be a pioneer if you don't pave new paths at some point.

Great philosophers and mentors want their students to surpass them, not be dependent on them. We should follow the examples of our pioneers, not their footsteps. Pioneers aren't traveling the one and only path to success there is. On the contrary, pioneers create multiple paths to success by having an expansive vision and being open to traveling uncharted territory. The blueprint for success that worked for one pioneer probably won't work for you because all pioneers walk unique paths. The best thing we can inherit from our pioneers is the mindset of **in-possibility (the belief that anything is possible).**

Great minds don't think alike. History only repeats itself because we have been conditioned to think alike instead of encouraging and accepting divergent thought. In psychology they call this group think. Group think is a type of thought exhibited by group members who try to minimize conflict and reach consensus without critically testing, analyzing, and evaluating all of the possible ideas. During group think, members of the group avoid promoting viewpoints outside the comfort zone of consensus thinking. **If the limitless process of brainstorming is limited, then surely innovation in your life and your company will be limited as well.**

The paths that pioneers carve aren't just physical or financial —they are neural, mental, internal, and within. You are creating new ways of thinking that represents your individual interpretation of reality. If we all thought exactly alike, the same problems would continue to manifest and intensify decade after decade. Perhaps this is what is happening and that is why we need more pioneers.

PROFESSIONAL PACE CARS

When new companies challenge the business models of incumbents, they tend to create better products and services and new possibilities and choices for the consumer. Examples include Apple's iPod and iPhone and the way they have fundamentally changed the music industry and mobile market. Another example is Netflix and the way it revolutionized the video rental market, expanding the market and stealing market share from Blockbuster and Hollywood Video by leveraging the internet to challenge the assumption that video rental stores are required to execute their business model. In business, this is called a disruptive technology. A disruptive technology is an innovation that creates a new and unexpected market by solving an old problem in a brand new way through challenging assumptions and applying a different set of principles.

In the book *Eating the Big Fish: How Challenger Brands Can Compete Against Brand Leaders,* the Eat Big Fish consulting firm lays out the thought process challenger brands need to have to grow in markets where incumbents have historically dominated. The process for creating a professional and organizational challenger brand is as follows:

1. List all of the assumptions your industry currently holds about success, execution, and its customers

2. Develop counter-thoughts that challenge those assumptions

3. Choose the top three counter-thoughts that may be true because of new technology or simply new times

4. Build your brand, positioning, and products with those principles in mind.

If you do what everyone else does, then you will end up exactly where everyone else ends up. Pioneers challenge "what is" with "what is yet to come" and this applies to individuals and companies alike.

FOLLOW TO LEAD

When following and learning from your pioneers, you should follow to eventually take the lead. Pioneers use their lives to pave one of many possible paths. Though potentially similar, their path is not your path. You must keep your eyes open to all possibilities instead of just focusing on the back bumpers of your pioneers. I've identified a few ways to follow pioneers, each with its own pros and cons.

COMPANY PROFILE:
PIONEERS & NETFLIX

In February of 2009, Netflix reached its 10 millionth subscriber mark. Since 1999, it has been focused on leveraging technology to get you what you want to watch faster, cheaper, and easier. By creating an online-based distribution model instead of a store-based one, Netflix could:

1. Capture valuable information about movies that Blockbuster couldn't with its physical drop box

2. Create community by allowing you to check out what your friends where watching, and

3. Create a powerful recommendation system that allows you to find you movies you might like

According to CNET, a leading website for product reviews, as of September 2006, Netflix.com had more than 5.7 million users while Blockbuster.com only had 1.5 million users. Clearly Netflix was ahead of the game and still is. Blockbuster is slowly transitioning and trying to create a value proposition that leverages its 9,000 stores nationwide instead of closing them. Since 2006, Blockbuster's stock price has decreased by 81% (3.87 to .72) while Netflix has grown 199% (23.47 to 46.60).

While Blockbuster tires to play catch up online, Netflix has to continue thinking like a pioneer as YouTube and Hulu play in similar spaces and On Demand TV becomes more affordable and available.

Caravan: Caravanning is a monkey-see-monkey-do style of driving. This is like an apprenticeship, where you watch the pioneer drive from their passenger seat until they eventually teach you how to drive like them and let you take the wheel. Oftentimes, family businesses operate like this. When I was getting my driver's license, I realized that there was no substitute for practicing driving except to actually drive myself. Hopefully you have a trusting relationship in which your pioneer allows you to take the wheel and make mistakes as they ride as your passenger and instructor. Another challenge is that you may not get a chance to lead until your pioneer lets go of the wheel.

Pacesetter: In long distance running, the concept of the pacesetter is common. They usually jump out and take the lead and others stay close behind until they feel that it is time to strike. If your pioneer speeds up, you speed up. If they slow down, you slow down. That's why in marathons you don't see a lot of lead changes until the end of the race. Up until that point in time, people are conserving their energy for the final stretch by just keeping up with the pace setter. **In the marathon of life this can be a good strategy, but it's unlikely that you will break any world records if you adjust to someone else's pace—unless they are trying to break a world record too.**

Alternative: Traffic only happens when you're following the band, so an alternative is to strategically allow them to go first, learn from them, and then do the opposite. **Since everyone doesn't follow a particular pioneer for one reason or another, there must be people who disagree or are indifferent that may follow your lead.** If there is a group of people who like low cost goods, there is likely a group of people that value high cost good. Contrarians challenge long-held assumptions that shake the foundation of their sphere of influence. Contrarian thinking is the impetus behind the success of many well-known companies. Google would not be Google without Yahoo! being a pioneer in online search. Google challenged Yahoo's model of paying people to index the Internet by creating an alternate algorithm to gauge a site's relevance based on a number of factors, like links. **Contrarians figure out what the herd is doing and do the exact opposite and that is how they discover their niche or new market.**

A healthy mixture of each style of following is good. The style you choose depends heavily on your relationship with the pioneer (i.e. proximity, trust, etc). It's easy to walk a path that has already been paved, but we all have a unique path and contribution to make to ourselves, other people, our companies and this world. Therefore, at some point your path has to branch off to create new possibilities and ideas.

By challenging the underlying principles of previously successful pioneers, you can create alternatives to your present way of being that creates more possibilities for yourself and others. There is a saying that "what got you here won't get you there," meaning that what made them successful today may not make you successful tomorrow. Naturally, when someone is successful they think it is because of what they are currently doing and therefore want to stick to that, but in reality, success comes from constantly evolving and embodying a certain combination of skills and characteristics at a particular moment in time. **Nature is perhaps the best model of sustainable success, and She succeeds through constant evolution—a never-ending process of dying, adapting, and creating anew.** When observing your pioneers, you can use a contrarian's eye to see assumptions, obstacles, and opportunities that they can't or didn't see.

CONCLUSION

Your guides may have walked similar paths, but no one has walked your path. Exposure to other people's paths and stories will open your mind to new ones. You should honor your pioneers for their character and personal growth and less so for their particular paths and social achievements. **Some people leave their mark on the world and other people leave dents. In order to leave a dent you have to create your own i-dent-ity (an authentic way of living that inevitably shapes the world because of its authenticity).**

As children, the concept of monkey-see-monkey-do was how we learned. We watched someone else and tried to mimic them. Instead of saying "I want to be like...," you should just say "I want to be..." and then finish the sentence with your own imagination instead of a person's name. **It is impossible to try to be "like" someone while at the same time do things they never did. The "me-too" mentality will lead you to take paths that you think have made others successful, when in fact, the only path you will succeed on is your own.**

The question I always ask myself when I think about my life is "Am I keeping mapmakers in business?" If I'm not changing the landscape of life, then no new maps need to be made and thus mapmakers go out of business. If I am pushing frontiers, I am charting new courses and paving new roads, thus mapmakers will always have jobs as long as I'm alive. The chapter on pioneers naturally precedes the chapter on picture because pioneers map uncharted areas. Maps only chart where someone has already been but pioneers step off the page of the map and expand it. Pioneers keep mapmakers in business with their new discoveries and innovations. If the landscape of life never changed, we would only need one map forever. New realizations lead to new roads and new innovations lead to new highways. Since each individual has their own path to pave, everyone should have their own street name because there should be as many roads as there are unique people.

UNCHARTED TERRITORY
PERSONAL PIONEERS

Directions: Write a thank you note to one of your personal pioneers expressing why you think they are a pioneer, and how they change you and the world through their journey. They can be alive or deceased or an individual or an organization. If they are an individual who is alive, I encourage you to send it to them.

Dear..,

Thank you for being a pioneer...

....

....

....

....

....

....

....

Sincerely,

PROFESSIONAL PIONEERS

Directions: Identify one of your path-specific pioneers and the lanes they occupied and map out where they began, where they ended, and how you plan to take it further. Secondly, list some assumptions from your lane or industry and write alter-native viewpoints that challenge the old way of thinking.

Pioneer Name:..

Lane/Industry/Skill:..

Where did the lane end when they started?

....

....

Where and how did they pave a new road?

....

....

Where and how do you envision taking the road further?

....

....

ASSUMPTIONS & ALTERNATIVES

ASSUMPTIONS/ RULES IN MY LANE	ALTERNATIVE/ CHALLENGING VIEWPOINTS
Example: Personal development is personal	*Example: Personal development works best in groups*
Assumption 1	Alter-native Viewpoint 1
Assumption 2	Alter-native Viewpoint 2
Assumption 3	Alter-native Viewpoint 3
Assumption 4	Alter-native Viewpoint 4

MOVE-MEANT

Where The Rubber Meets The Road

Below are specific actions you can do in the next 30 days to align your life a little bit more with your personal and professional pioneers.

Personal: Identify three personal pioneers. If your personal pioneers are still alive, interview them about their journeys. If not, ask other people who knew them and write down why you think they were pioneers and identify the characteristics of a pioneer based on your interviews.

Professional: Identify three professional pioneers. Feel free to use the Internet to find out as much information as possible about them. Look for similarities and differences in their lives. Become versed on who they were, why they were, and what they envisioned. Create your own criteria on what it takes to be a pioneer in your profession. Professional pioneers can be individuals or companies.

PICTURE »
YOUR ROAD MAP

THE PURPOSE OF THIS CHAPTER IS TO:

- Release any tunnel visions and identify blind spots you may have
- Create a holistic vision of potential possibilities for your life

GUIDING QUEST-IONS:

Personal: What's my vision for myself and my world?

Professional: What's my company's vision for our organization and the world? What's my company's vision for my career?

QUOTES:

"We must be willing to get rid of the life we planned so as to have the life that is waiting for us."
— Joseph Campbell

"Dream lofty dreams, and as you dream, so you shall become. Your vision is the promise of what you shall one day be; your ideal is the prophecy of what you shall at last unveil."
— James Allen

WILL SMITH'S VISION: MOVIE STAR

When I think about vision, the first person to come to mind is Will Smith. His road map took him from *hot* raps about "Summertime" to *The Fresh Prince of Bel-Air* to becoming one of the biggest movie star in the world. According to Forbes, he grossed $80 million in 2008 with *I Am Legend*, *Pursuit of Happyness*, and *Hancock*. In a December 2007 article with Straight.com, Smith discusses how he and his agent planned for success:

"I said, 'I want to be the biggest movie star in the world,' and he said that we should probably figure out what they do and plot a course. We went out and rented the top-10 movies of all time and we tried to figure out the patterns. We could see that every film in the top 10 had special effects and that nine were special effects with creatures and eight added a love story to that formula. So the 1996 action film Independence Day was not a difficult choice to make."

According to Movieweb.com's "All Time Top 1000 Grossing Movies List" those movies include:

1. *Titanic*
2. *Dark Knight*
3. *Star Wars: Episode 4*
4. *Shrek 2*
5. *E.T.*
6. *Star Wars: Episode 1*
7. *Pirates of the Caribbean: Dead Man's Chest*
8. *Spider Man*
9. *Star Wars: Episode 3*
10. *Lord of the Rings: The Return of the King*

Based on the formula Smith derived by studying pioneers, it was no coincidence that he went after the Independence Day role in 1996, leaving Bel-Air behind after the 146th episode of a show that lasted six years, between 1990 and 1996. Many of his lead roles in movies paint vivid pictures of destruction and Armageddon such as *Independence Day, I Am Legend, and Men In Black*. And yet in his real life, Will Smith paints an uplifting vision for himself and is realizing more and more of that vision with every film. He doesn't just star in *motion pictures*—his life is a *picture in motion*.

MY PICTURE: A GENERATION'S INSPIRATION

My first exposure to visioning was sports. At age 11, just as the regular baseball season ended and we transitioned into all-stars, my baseball coach taught me about visioning. He read all kinds of books about hitting and one of them talked about visioning and imagining a successful at-bat before it even happens. During the 45-minute drive to a regional all-star tournament, I would close my eyes and imagine myself in the batter's box getting solid hits in every gap in the infield and outfield. After batting over .800 (8 hits for every 10 at-bats) in the tournament, I was convinced about this process. Granted this was little league baseball, even Ty Cobb, the all-time best hitter in major league baseball, only batted .366.

I was the smallest and fastest man on the basketball court so I was always designated point guard. As point guard, I was coached to develop my peripheral vision, so that I could see passing lanes and teammates without looking directly at the player to whom I intended to pass the ball. In basketball, they use the term "court vision"—meaning you are simultaneously aware of the entire court as well as the defender in front of you. A guard with court vision is able to see opportunities for themselves and their teammates at all times.

Though sports faded out of my vision in high school, I took the visioning process with me. Visioning manifested in my life through two writing exercises I will never forget. The first was my Stanford MBA admissions essay and the prompt was, "What matters to you most and why?" A book I read prompted me to write my eulogy from the perspective of my best friend inspired the second exercise. The Stanford essay made me consider my "why" based on where my life took me thus far and the eulogy demanded that I travel backwards down memory lane as if I had already reached the end. Both writing prompts challenged me to look within myself and examine what I believed was possible for my life.

At the end of the chapter, I encourage you to write a eulogy or a 80th birthday toast and a re-tire-meant speech to capture your vision for your life and how you want to be remembered. To ensure that your vision is holistic, be sure to include vivid pictures of your educational, financial, spiritual, physical, professional, and familial life. You can find my Stanford Graduate School of Business admissions essay and my eulogy online at www.julliengordon.com.

PICTURE AS ROAD MAP

Your picture is a road map of the landscape of life based on what you *know is possible* whereas, your imagine-nation is what you *believe is possible*. Your road map has limits and ends where the image ends; your mental map ends where your imagine-nation ends. However, the difference between what one *knows* and what one *believes* can be strikingly different for two people based on their exposure and experiences. What you know comes from your personal experiences and awareness of other's experiences. As your awareness expands, your road map and mental map expand proportionally.

In geometry, we were taught that a line is the most direct route between two points. In life, the most direct way isn't always the best way, especially if everyone thinks that the most direct way is the best way. Though I've never understood traffic, I'm certain that the "direct is best" belief contributes to its formation. **There are many people trying to get to the same place in life, but it doesn't mean that the best route for one type of driver in one type of vehicle is the best route for all drivers and all vehicles.**

When getting directions using the Internet you have to put in your origin (where you are) and your destine-nation (where you want to go). All you have to do is click the "get directions" button and your plan is laid out for you down to the minute and the turn. It's easy to plan a road trip because you're 99% certain that the roads on the directions you print will be there. But the same certainty doesn't hold true in life. Today, the landscape of life is changing so fast that the roads we plan to take to get where we want to go are not guaranteed to be there. You can only prepare for the 99% uncertain future ahead, though 99% certainty is preferred. Even the green freeway signs hanging over every other overpass only state the next 3 exits ahead. **Therefore, it is more important to hold firm to your *direction* rather than a set of *directions*.**

Most people think that if they have directions, they don't need a map, but I would rather have a map than directions if

205

I were lost or misdirected. Directions don't account for detours or delays. **Directions are like plans, they only represent the single most common path to get where you want to go. Plans rarely account for error or change. Like directions, plans are usually sequential and if there happens to be an unexpected detour, the plan becomes useless.** There is a difference between having a picture of where you want to go and knowing how to get there. Having a picture adds texture to what you hope for while a plan outlines how to get to where you hope. Without starting with a destine-nation in mind, the only possible plan to create is a plan to nowhere fast.

A top-level view of the landscape of life allows you to see where you are in relation to where you want to go, similar to how you can't see what a helicopter can see sitting inside of your vehicle. A road map gives you a helicopter view of the past, present, and future. Your road map allows you visualize the destine-nation, but it doesn't define a particular way to get there. There are infinite ways to get to a particular destine-nation on the road and in life. Directions are very limited and narrow, but a map gives you a birds-eye view of the entire landscape. Even when street names stop looking familiar, you can refer to a map to identify where you are, where you want to go, and many ways to get there.

The clearer our picture is of our destine-nation, the easier it is to navigate detours, delays, and wrong directions. There are guaranteed to be obstacles in life that require you to think on the fly while still having your destine-nation in mind. While most people get caught in traffic in their professional and personal lives, a clear picture of the landscape of life allows you to think outside of the box of your car and see life from the perspective of the helicopter that reports traffic.

Traffic comes and goes, but a birds-eye-view of life helps you see the best path to take without being limited by your own windshield, mirrors, and blind spots. **When you focus on your vision instead of a specific plan or route, you may find what you're looking for faster in a place you didn't expect. It's like being en route to the ATM you always go to and along the way stumbling upon a new one or one you've been overlooking because you've been so focused on your way in the past.**

Your picture is one of many possible mental images or visions of where you want to be and how your being affects the world. It is your ideal state for the entire world without implying any lack, emptiness, or unhappiness in your life at this moment. **Your picture has more to do with *who* you want to be than *how* you plan to be that. It's about the change in you, not the change outside of you.** Though it seems like your picture is out in the in the distant future, the only way to become who you want to be later is to move towards being that person now. You must align your trajectory with the person you want to be. Those who don't shape their own trajectory lead tragic lives. You approach your vision and align your trajectory with your purpose through your daily choices and actions.

PERSONAL ROAD MAP

Imagine putting a puzzle together. Your picture or vision is like the box. The image on the box doesn't tell you how to put the puzzle together, but it gives you some *direction* (as opposed to specific *directions*). There is a significant distinction between direction and directions: direction creates space for exploration and uncertainty whereas directions are inflexible. It's rare to see someone attempt to put a puzzle together without looking at the image on the box.

Through conducting timed races on 60-piece puzzles, I was surprised to observe that the people without a box actually finish quicker than people with the box. Those without the box are scrappier and move faster piece-by-piece in comparison to the people with the box who spend their time planning and matching according to the box. The person with the plan might look prettier and more organized in their actions, but the person who scraps tends to finish first. If the vision or the box is too firm, it becomes like a set of directions. So if there happens to be a missing piece, frustration sets in because things aren't going as planned. Meanwhile the person without the box keeps trying new pieces with no consciousness that a piece may be missing and gets through the puzzle by trial and error. They move with the awareness that they don't know the answer and are therefore able to learn while the people with the box move as if they know the final answer and are closed off to anything that doesn't match their picture.

The puzzle box isn't useless, it just needs to be used properly. The visioning process is an art that requires beginning with the end in mind. In the same way that we look to the puzzle box for general direction when putting it back together, visioning is essential to help you map out the unconnected dots of your life. In his 2005 commencement speech at Stanford University, Steve Jobs, founder of Apple Inc. said:

"You can't connect the dots looking forward; you can only connect them looking backwards. So you have to trust that the dots will somehow connect in your future. You have to trust in something — your gut, destiny, life, karma, whatever.

This approach has never let me down, and it has made all the difference in my life."

Vision is what connects the dots and themes in our lives. The purpose of visioning is to step outside of yourself and mentally go to the place you want to be, so that you can travel backward in your mind in order to get an idea of how to get where you want to go from where you currently are.

Vision is a 3-step process that pulls from your past, present, and future. It requires weaving pieces of your life together to create a new life. The three steps include: clearing, collaging, and creating.

1. Clearing what was:

Before you begin visioning, you must first let go and erase our notions of "what was" and start with a clean slate. It's impossible to vision on a painted canvas. When it comes to changing ourselves individually or collectively, a lot of people say things like, "It's always been like that," but deep in our hearts, we know that nothing is permanent and that our lives only make up a fraction of eternity. We tend to hold onto that which we are comfortable with, whether it is good or bad for us. We hold onto the past, the past doesn't hold on to us. The past has passed. You have the power to let go of the past and start anew whenever you choose. This requires forgiving yourself, releasing regrets and sometimes people so that you can move forward.

2. Collaging with what is:

Collaging is a process that is typically associated with cutting things out of a magazine and gluing them onto a poster board. The process works the same in a non-literal sense—pulling ideas, images, and words together to make a cohesive idea. Books like *The Secret* have demonstrated the power of visioning and more people are creating vision boards to help them attract the life they want to live. Once you have a clearing, you can use collaging to pull from different pieces of your experiences that you love and want more of, and add those to your vision. Most vision boards tend to focus on the materials people want to have (i.e. houses, cars, spouse), but a purpose-filled vision board should focus on characteristics that one wants to embody (i.e. leadership, good health, peace). What's the point of having what you want if you can't be your authentic self while having it? **A purpose-filled vision board is about *being who you want to be* versus just *having what you want to have*, which often means it has more words and phrases than images of things unless they are symbolic of who you want to be. New things can't come to you if you're not willing to change who you are being and what you're doing.**

3. Creating what is yet to be:

Creation is still taking place every moment. The creation story didn't end at the last page of Genesis or the Big Bang. Every moment is an opportunity to create a new world. You have the power to shape your future with every thought, word, and action. Central to my vision board is the quote "The best way to predict the future is to create it." You can use your imagine-nation to create new images, ideas, and possibilities that you've never seen before and bring forth "what is yet to be" through your life. This way of visioning is characteristic of pioneers. They look at what was and what is and then create what is yet to be.

PROFESSIONAL ROAD MAP

In August of 2006, a team of Colorado educators developed a powerful presentation about globalization and its impact on American education. The online PowerPoint presentation called "Shift Happens" vividly articulates the rapid rate by which the world is evolving professionally, technologically, and academically. Some striking statistics include:

• China will soon become the #1 English-speaking country in the world.
• The U.S. Department of Labor estimates that today's worker will have 10-14 jobs by the age of 38.
• According to former Secretary of Education Richard Riley, the top 10 in-demand jobs in 2010 did not exist in 2004. In other words, we are educating kids for jobs that won't be there when they become employable.
• With 106 million users, if MySpace.com were a country, it would be the 11th largest country in the world between Japan and Mexico.
• More that 3,000 new books are published every day.
• Half of what students learn in their first year of study will be outdated by their third year of study.

There is no sign of these trends slowing down. Therefore, we must learn to get comfortable with change and uncertainty and let go of our time lines. Proverbs 29:18 says, "A people without a vision will perish," not a people without a plan. Like driving directions, detailed plans look great on paper, but can also be limiting. On the other hand, a vision is an inspiring image of the future that leaves all possible routes to get there open.

THE CAREER TRANSITION TEST

As you create a picture for you career, you should assess whether or not your current company is the best place for you to realize that vision. Regardless of what industry you're in, you may want to ask yourself the following questions to determine if it's time to transition before the shift that is happening happens to you and your career:

1. Is my industry currently growing or dying?
2. When was the last major innovation or turn of events? Historically, how often do they tend to happen?
3. What innovative idea may destroy or resurrect my industry?
4. How innovative has my company been in leading and dealing with change?
5. Who or what trends and technologies should my company have their eye on? Why?
6. Will my company be an industry leader in 3-5 years? If not, then who will be?

Pioneering companies make pioneering people. They cultivate and preserve cultures that encourage free thinking where great minds are actually allowed to think different. They allow for smart risks to be taken because educated risks are the seeds of innovation. Therefore, if you want to have a career that can move an entire company and industry in a new direction, then it is essential to be in a company that believes in its employees, encourages free-thinking, and has already demonstrated that it has been a pioneer more than once through its products, services, and culture. PayPal is a great example of this. After being bought out by eBay, PayPal's former employees went on to found YouTube, LinkedIn, and Yelp. One of the best ways to evaluate an employer is by the career trajectory of its alumni or former employees.

In 2009, buzz words like recession, foreclosure, and unemployment infected the media. On January 26, 2009, 76 thousand jobs were lost in one day. Caterpillar laid off 20 thousand, Pfizer 19 thousand, Sprint 8 thousand, and Home Depot 7 thousand among others. That's how quickly jobs, businesses, and industries can evaporate. But job loss is not the only issue. Underemployment and job creation are the other parts of the economic equation. Every industry and company has cash inflow and outflow just like every river has inflow and outflow. It's just a natural part of business cycle and life. Industries grow from nothing more than an idea in someone's head and then they die just like people. Nothing is permanent.

You can't seriously plan your life and career more than 6 months in advance, however, you can always hold your vision. There will be new roads, detours, potholes, and accidents as the world shifts to ensure its own survival and your growth. New forms of employment (such as the green industry) will emerge and old knowledge and forms of education will die as new ones are born. By planning too much, you cut yourself off to possibilities you cannot see yet because you haven't been exposed to them, they have yet to be created, or you have yet to create them. **Vision is the *end state* while goals are the short road trips from *state-to-state*. Only after defining the end state can you develop meaningful goals.**

We live in a world that focuses on the quantity of life instead of the quality. If a man walks 2,000 miles in a 1-mile circle while another man walks 2,000 miles in a straight line, who

COMPANY PROFILE:
PICTURE & GOOGLE

Beginning as a class project in 1996, Larry Page and Sergey Brin went on to create world's best search engine, Google. It was fast, accurate and easy to use. According to their corporate history, they named the company Google as a play on the word "googol," a mathematical term for the number represented by the numeral 1 followed by 100 zeros. This term reflected their vision and mission to organize the world's information and make it universally accessible and useful. Since then, Google has expanded into a variety of products and services that leverage their core competency for search, such as Gmail and Google Maps.

Google is always thinking ahead and envisioning the future. Their futurist mindset is captured in three principles within the Google Philosophy:

5. You don't need to be at your desk to need an answer.

They believe that the world is increasingly mobile and that people are not tied to fixed locations, and thus create new products and services that address this trend.

7. There's always more information out there.

They believe that HTML pages are just the beginning and as a result have expanded into e-mail, maps, stocks, health, video, news, books, and images.

8. The need for information crosses all borders.

They believe that English is great, but customization in 35 more languages is even better despite new challenges in search technology that arise because of language differences.

In addition, all Google engineers are allowed to spend 20% of their time on projects and creative visions or quest-ions they have in hopes that they will discover new ways to achieve their mission. A lot of people only know Google for their search engine, but they have a full range of products designed to increase the flow of accurate information worldwide. Had Google not create the Ad Words revenue model, they could have easily ended up being an amazing non-profit like Wikipedia, but their 6th philosophy states, "You can make money without doing evil" and they have proven it. Though few people categorize Google as a social entrepreneurial venture, I believe that they are the best model of social entrepreneurship to date, making substantial money while also helping the world.

has traveled further? Though they traveled the same distance, we tend to respect the man who walked straight because of the perception that he went somewhere. At the end of the day, both men have traveled the same distance. The real question is "Who enjoyed their journey most?" despite where they each ended up. I remember setting aggressive timelines for myself like, "I want to be a millionaire and retire by 35" or "I want to get married by 30." But then I realized that my timelines weren't based on anything except an arbitrary age I randomly selected to achieve those milestones. What's the rush? **I call these ego-als. They are lofty goals that sound fly like eagles but are primarily ego-driven.** Your vision will manifest at the rate that you focus your energy directly on achieving them and everything needed to support the manifestation of your purpose will be supplied to you.

TYPES OF VISION

Your vision reflects the number of possibilities you think are available to you at any given moment. When driving, we use three types of vision: tunnel vision, rear-view vision, and peripheral vision. Two drivers can be driving on the same road and experience it differently. A driver with tunnel vision could be frustrated at the car in front of them because that's all they see, whereas someone with peripheral vision can see the flow of traffic ahead and navigate accordingly.

Tunnel vision: Tunnel vision is when you only see one way out of a situation. You feel limited and confined with no ability to escape. Whether it is the medical student who doesn't like medicine but did it to make their parents happy or the dedicated employee whose entire identity is wrapped up in their career and company, there is always another way. The tunnel walls aren't real. People with tunnel vision can expand their limited view of the world by breaking down the tunnel walls created by their academic degrees, other people's expectations, and the fear of being behind. At that point, they will realize that there is never just one way and their vision will expand from "what I think I have to do" to "what I truly want to do."

Rear view vision: Rear view vision has to do with leveraging pride or shame from the past to shape your future. When you live in the past, you aren't fully present in the now, which is the only moment that there is and thus the only moment that truly matters. Shame is like heavy baggage that you can use to make excuses about why you aren't as far along on your journey as you think you should be. As discussed in the Problems chapter, we must find creative ways to use personal pain to motivate or else it will just hold us back. Though personal success isn't viewed negatively like personal shame, it can be just as dangerous. When people rest on their laurels or what they achieved in the past, they tend to become complacent and end up losing their edge. **The safest way to drive is to be fully present in the moment regardless of past success or failure, treating every moment like its your last.**

Peripheral vision: Peripheral vision allows you to see other possibilities while still focusing on what's in front of you. It expands your options and awareness of reality. Unlike tunnel vision, a person using peripheral vision is open to the possibility of change and is flexible. **They aren't restricted to a particular path. Instead they let the best path reveal itself to them by keeping their options open.** As stated before, the void is where the value is, and peripheral vision allows one to see gaps in the flow of traffic and forge new paths to avoid the congestion. The driver's side and passenger's window give them a 180 degree view of the world ahead and around them, while a person with tunnel vision is limited to their immediate situation and a person with rear view vision is limited by the past.

All three types of visions are necessary in life, but the size of each mirror is no accident. The windshield is bigger than the rear view mirror intentionally. Imagine having a rear-view mirror the size of your windshield and a windshield the size of your rear view mirror. You would be stuck in the past. Your windshield is bigger than your rear view mirror because you're supposed to drive looking forward. When you are changing lanes, it is good to briefly look in your rear view to see what may be coming up from your past, but overall, your vision needs to be in the present and in the periphery.

CONCLUSION

Despite the fact that visioning has no constraints, we still limit and doubt ourselves. Because we don't know ourselves, we are unaware of our potential, and therefore we limit what we are capable of. One of my mentors told me that if people don't laugh at you when you share your vision, then it's probably not big enough. If they don't laugh, then they obviously think that you are already capable of becoming what you envision. That suggests that you are thinking too small and not challenging yourself to think off the map. Failure occurs when you test your limitations but because of failure's negative perception, people choose to recline in comfort instead. **Failure is simply success at something you didn't intend to succeed at. When you authentically go after what you believe in, you often fail forward meaning that you don't get what you initially intend—**

instead you end up with something better. Those who don't fail aren't pushing any boundaries. It's not until you push yourself to your limits that you realize you are limitless.

There is no official map, except that which pioneers have created. And even that gets outdated quickly because the landscape of life is changing at a very fast pace. What worked for them may not work for you. **Sometimes external factors like the weather affect our vision and make it difficult to drive, but more accidents in life are caused by lack of vision internally than obstructions of vision externally.** When you define what you want and are attracted to, the Law of Attraction begins to work in your favor. When you aren't clear on your vision, it's like having tinted windows and a dirty windshield—it's hard for you to see out and for others to see into you.

EULOGY OR TOAST

Directions: Write a eulogy or a toast to yourself from the perspective of your best friend when you're 80 years old. Questions to consider include:

- What roles do I envision myself taking on throughout my life? (i.e. parent, community leader, entrepreneur)
- What do I hope to leave behind? (i.e. family business, lasting change, my art, legacy)
- What's one word, belief, or quote that people will remember me for? Why? (i.e. honest, authentic, inspirational)

....

....

....

....

....

....

....

....

....

RE-TIRE-MEANT SPEECH

Directions: Imagine the last day of your career after 40 years of hard work. Finally, retirement! Write a short speech outlining the value you created, the legacy you left, the lives you impacted, the growth you sparked, and the change you brought about in your organization, industry, and world.

...... years and .... months from today, ..., ..., 20.....

....

....

....

....

....

....

....

....

....

MOVE-MEANT

Where The Rubber Meets The Road

Below are specific actions you can do in the next 30 days to align your life a little bit more with your personal and professional picture.

Personal: Identify three words from your eulogy, toast, or elsewhere that you want people to think of when they think of your character. Over the next month, do your best to embody those words and without mentioning the words, see how many people you can get to affirm you with those words or synonyms based on your presence and actions.

Professional: Identify three words from your re-tire-meant speech or elsewhere that you want to be remembered by in regards to your career. Over the next month, do your best to embody those words and without mentioning them, see how many people you can get to affirm you with those words or synonyms based on your presence and actions.

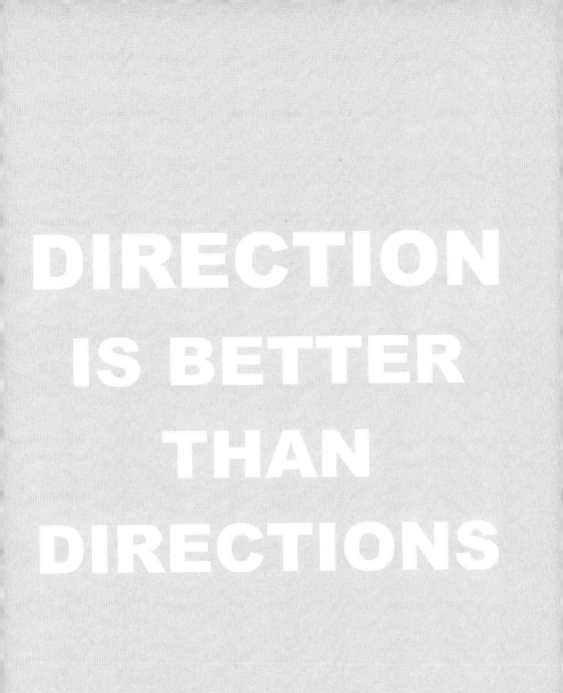

DIRECTION
IS BETTER
THAN
DIRECTIONS

POSSIBILITY »
YOUR DESTINATION

THE PURPOSE OF THIS CHAPTER IS TO:

* Identify what possibility you want to extend to the world with your life
* Differentiate between the concepts of options, possibilities, and in-possibility

GUIDING QUEST-IONS:

Personal: What's possible in the world *with* you that would not be possible *without* you?

Professional: What's possible in the world *with* my company that would not be possible *without* it? What is or will be possible for my company that wasn't possible before me?

QUOTES:

"Some men see things as they are and say 'Why?' I dream of things that never were and say 'Why not?'"
— George Bernard Shaw

"Man has the possibility of existence after death. But possibility is one thing and the realization of the possibility is quite a different thing."
— Bret Harte

MY POSSIBILITY: YOUR: IN-POSSIBILITY

Have you ever stared down the barrel of a gun? I remember the night vividly. It was Friday, June 15th, 2001, the night the Los Angeles Lakers won their first of three consecutive NBA champions under Phil Jackson with Shaquille O'Neal and Kobe Bryant. I was out with some friends promoting for an upcoming party we were throwing. I pulled into a dark parking lot to wait until the party was over so that we could distribute our flyers. As soon as I turned the car off, two men hopped out of a car in front of us with guns. One approached my door, while the other approached the rear door on the passenger side. I don't recall any words being exchanged. I stepped out, handed him the keys to my car, and off they drove.

That was my first car. It was a 12-year old 1989 Black 190E Mercedes Benz. I bought it at used car auction for cheap. I wanted to be like my parents who both had Mercedes Benzes. I wanted to show them that I was grown and on the path to doing better than them, like most parents hope for their kids. I worked tirelessly all summer at a batting cage and all throughout my first year of college as a tutor to buy that car. I had to put more money into the car to fix it than I did to buy it. My uncle used to tell me as a little boy, "Never buy anything that you can't maintain." I didn't understand what he meant until now. What made things worse was that I didn't have insurance when it was stolen.

Fortunately my car was the only thing they stole. In an instant, the gunman could have stolen my life. This story was my turning point and, ironically, without it I wouldn't be writing this book today. In addition to my own story, I noticed that car accidents were major turning points for many of my friends' lives, but I don't want you to have to face anything that severe to awaken you to your purpose. **Though I got carjacked, I realized that people are getting life-jacked every day. People's lives are being stolen with them sitting inside.** I believe that our lives are our vehicles to design, drive, and maintain, however, many people either end up backseat driving through life or driving other people's vehicles. Therefore, my possibility is to put you and millions of others back in the driver's seat of your own lives so that you can direct them in the way you want them to go.

POSSIBILITY AS DESTINATION

Paving a path to a new destine-nation that is physical, mental, social, or spiritual is the best way to leave a legacy. Life is not about choosing from an existing set of destine-nations and working to get there. Instead, you should be motivated by others' courage to create their own possibilities and then forge your own. **For most people, life is just a journey to buy enough gas to make it to the end.** After their engine burns out, their vehicle is worthless. Another way to view life is to see it as an opportunity to build momentum that will outlast the vehicle that creates it to benefit others. You can leave a legacy by using your life to maximize your personal velocity so that others can benefit from your energy. Your personal velocity dictates how far into the future your impact will last and you can increase that by living a purpose-filled life.

Since nobody has your destiny, your destine-nation is unique to you. But too often, we limit our destiny to a particular career path that can't contain the possibility that we are. A professional path is one avenue that you can use to reach your desired destine-nation, but it should never be the end goal. Creating new possibilities in your life, your organization, and the world should always be the primary focus and you should seek professional opportunities that allow you to do that. Even if where you are is great, there is always a way to make a better way. In the same way cars leave behind carbon footprints, when you exit Earth's Expressway, you will leave behind a carbon copy of yourself. If you create new possibilities for people through the vehicles of your life, work, or simply the way you live your life, the people that know you will have a road map to believe and follow until they are able to set out on their own road.

Life is short in comparison to eternity, so in reality, your life is just a series of moments that are strung together to create momentum that can shift the world beyond your physical existence. The momentum created by the lives of some of our spiritual leaders like Jesus Christ, Muhammad, and Buddha have lasted millennia, while scientists, innovators, and leaders like Henry Ford, Albert Einstein, and Martin Luther King Jr. impact centuries. **Everyone's life has an impact on the world whether small, big, negative, positive, short-term, or long-term. Through your actions, you have the power to determine how long your momentum will carry forward into the future, opening new possibilities for others that you never even experienced yourself.**

In-possible is the antonym of impossible. Impossibility is simply the poverty of possibility. Who can really say what is not possible? Though the imagination has no constraints, people are more quick to say what isn't possible with certainty than they are to say what may be possible. **If we had the opportunity to make a list of everything we**

could possibly want in the world, even if we wrote down everything we could think of, our list would only make up a tiny fraction of what is actually possible. There are three types of possibilities;

1. **Infinite Possibility:** The possibilities that are unknown or we don't believe in (infinite possibility).
2. **Our Picture:** The possibilities we think there are
3. **Our Options:** The possibilities we think are available to us

TYPES OF POSSIBILITIES

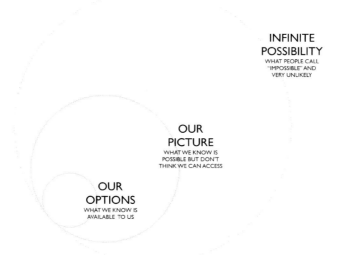

INFINITE
POSSIBILITY
WHAT PEOPLE CALL
"IMPOSSIBLE" AND
VERY UNLIKELY

OUR
PICTURE
WHAT WE KNOW IS
POSSIBLE BUT DON'T
THINK WE CAN ACCESS

OUR
OPTIONS
WHAT WE KNOW IS
AVAILABLE TO US

You never know everything that's possible because the future is 100% uncertain, but you can picture things that might change about you and the world as you embark on your journey. Searching for purpose is the process of discovering what is in-possible in the world *with* you that is impossible *without* you. Possibility is relative. What's impossible to you may seem impossible to someone else. Two people contemplating the same future will usually have varying levels of belief regarding the possibility of that future actually manifesting. But whatever your vision of the future is, create it.

PERSONAL DESTINATIONS

A lot of people see life like it's just a drive-thru. They choose from a pre-selected list of options, pay with their time and money, and expect to have it their way at the same time. If the current menu doesn't satisfy you, then you have to be committed enough to create exactly what you want in your life. Creation is a more effective use of your energy than complaining. Though life operates in cycles, history should never repeat itself. Instead of a circle that retraces itself, think of the cycle of life as an expanded Slinky that spirals upward. History only repeats itself because we haven't created new possibilities for the world, therefore we are limited to the old menu of options and the way things have been. History has no back cover because my story and your story are still being written by our lives. **If the world is going to change, we as individuals must change. If I'm going to change the world, I need a world of change in me.**

It's one thing to make change *in* the world and it's another to make change *on* it. We need soul-utions that transform the soul, not just solutions that transform the surface. Change in the world means tapping into the spiritual source from which creation and all possibility comes to create something new. Though many believe there is nothing new under the sun, that doesn't mean we've fully explored all the possibilities out there and in us. Change on the world means taking what already exists and simply moving some pieces around hoping that everything will be better. Soul-utions move us into the realm of infinite possibility—a possibility we can't imagine or see that grows organically out of people committing to their unique purposes.

At the end of the journey, you will have traveled from one version of yourself and arrived at a new you. In transforming yourself, you've also transformed the world as you learn to drive with your *in-sight*, not your *eyesight*. Writer and painter, Henry Miller, once said, "One's destination is never a place, but a new way of seeing things." In order to drive the world forward in a positive direction, you must be able to see what nobody else sees and go where no one else has gone. By aligning your 8 Cylinders of Success and moving in faith, you can live a purpose-filled life that moves and inspires others to live purpose-filled lives, which generates a cycle of liberated beings that ultimately extricates us all from the cycle we call history.

Throughout this internal journey, we have inspected the eight parts of your life that are essential to align in order to live the most purpose-filled life possible. We have defined:

1. What success means (Principles),
2. What ignites you (Passions),
3. What fuels you (Problems),
4. What motivates you (People),
5. Which lane is best for you (Positioning),
6. Who is leading you (Pioneers),
7. What the road map looks like (Picture), and
8. What new destine-nations you create with your life (Possibility).

Now that your inspection is done, all you need to do is step inside your vehicle and drive. The word vehicle has many definitions that can help us understand the purpose of our lives. Essentially, your body is your vehicle and it is designed to carry you where your purpose leads. Even if our Man-you-fact-urers are different, all cars are made from the same material. Our make and model is human being. When the parts of your life are in perfect a-line-meant and functioning as one, you will be able to advance yourself and the world forward in a powerful way.

PROFESSIONAL DESTINATIONS

Career transitioning is becoming more and more frequent and the best way to tell your story to future employers is by communicating what you made possible at your previous organization. You should never leave any organization without leaving a positive legacy of some sort. Your resume should not be a cut-copy-paste of your job description. It should be written as the legacy you left behind at your old job, describing where the organization was when you joined it and the new destine-nation you helped it arrive at through your work. There is a stark difference between a resume bullet-point saying:

- "I created and executed the nationwide marketing strategy"

  and

- "I shortened the marketing season from 7 months to 3.5 months while simultaneously increasing our customer base by 25% nationwide."

DEFINITIONS & APPLICATIONS OF VEHICLE

DICTIONARY DEFINITION OF THE WORD VEHICLE	APPLICATION OF THE DEFINITION TO YOU
1. Any means in or by which someone travels or something is carried or conveyed; a means of conveyance or transport: a motor vehicle; space vehicles.	You have all the means you need to carry or convey the message of your purpose.
2. A conveyance moving on wheels, runners, tracks, or the like, as a cart, sled, automobile, or tractor.	Your body is the vehicle that moves you through the world. However, instead of moving on *wheels*, your *will* moves you.
3. A means of transmission or passage: Air is the vehicle of sound.	You are a vehicle for your Man-you-fact-urer to transmit itself in the world.
4. A carrier, as of infection.	You are a carrier of a unique purpose that can positively infect the world.
5. A medium of communication, expression, or display: The novel is a fitting vehicle for his talents. Language is the vehicle of thought.	You are the medium through which your Man-you-fact-urer expresses itself in the world.
6. Theater, Movies. a play, screenplay, or the like, having a role suited to the talents of and often written for a specific performer.	You have a script written just for you that is suited to your talents and 8 Cylinders of Success
7. A means of accomplishing a purpose: College is a vehicle for success.	Your pursuit of purpose will lead you to success and happiness

The first bullet-point articulates what I did while the second one captures the value I created which is more important than what I did on a daily basis. I call this the A-to-B resume because it describes how you moved your past organizations from some point-A to some point-B. It speaks to your personal and professional velocity and the value you created in a way that your job description can't do on its own. If you enter employment with the mindset of legacy-building, an organization will offer you more money when you try to leave. And if you decide to leave, your new potential employer won't question why because they will be so focused on wanting you rather than looking for reasons not to hire you.

Each time we transition careers is like a mini re-tire-meant. Re-tire-meant has been glorified by society as the period of life where happiness begins. Though re-tire-meant typically happens around age 65, young people are rushing to retire early. The mere concept of looking forward to re-tire-meant suggests that we don't look forward to the work we do every day. Whether you're following your passions or not, work is hard. Usually if work is too easy, we are getting taxed in other ways that are hard to account for, like stress or unhappiness. Happiness is not some future state based on what happens in one's life. Happiness can only be experienced in the present moment. Why put off something for tomorrow that you can experience today? The moment you start living on purpose is the moment you retire from jobs. The only real retirement is the end of this life itself or the transition of one purpose to another purpose in the same life time.

Purpose transcends profession, but your career path is one avenue to express your purpose. Purpose should not be

COMPANY PROFILE:
POSSIBILITY &
THE DEPARTMENT OF MOTIVATED VEHICLES

I can't speak to the possibility of a company that I'm not a part of so I'll speak to the possibility of the Department of Motivated Vehicles (DMV). The DMV is a personal and professional development company committed to inspiring millions to live their daily lives in alignment with their passions and purpose. We help individuals through the toughest transitions of their lives such as college-to-career, career-to-career, and career-to-college by creating transformational group experience that help people discover and align their lives with their purpose.

We help organizations increase productivity, engagement, and retention of employees by clarifying the organization's purpose and each employee's purpose within that larger purpose so that intrinsic and extrinsic motivation is maximized. Since 2005 we have served over a thousand people and dozens of organizations through motivation teaching, motivational speaking, innovative courses, HR consulting, curriculum development, and life and executive coaching.

We want to use the life of our company to create in-possibilities in the lives of people, organizations, and industries that transcend our imagination. Ultimately, we are creating a self-fulfilling community and movement of the most powerful fleet of living vehicles with the collective capacity to move the world in the direction they wish.

confined to a position or sacrificed for a paycheck. As you engage in the employment process—the exchange of your time for money—you should beware aware that earning money can be extremely expensive in non-financial ways if it costs you your dreams. For every opportunity to earn a dollar, you exchange time. **Time is your most valuable resource. No amount of money can buy a second of time. Time is priceless. The most valuable way to spend your most valuable resource is doing what you value.** Through your purposes, you create unique value in the world. As your awareness of your purpose and unique value heightens, you will be able to create more value and capture it financially, thus being fed by your purpose as you feed it.

TURN YES, TURN NO

Now that you've found clarity on where you are and where you want to go, the next step is how to get there. They say if you fail to plan then you plan to fail, but, if you plan too much you fail to move and experience. How to get there won't necessarily be some elaborate plan. Instead, it will likely be a series of successive, moment-to-moment, yes or no decisions made with the awareness of your purpose or GPS system to guide you to the right choices.

On this journey of life, there are only two choices at each crossroad— yes or no. Every day we make thousands of yes or no decisions, some consciously and others unconsciously. After waking up in the morning, we probably make at least 300 choices before leaving our bedroom. The mere process of choosing what we're going to wear every day consists of saying no to every shirt in your closet except the one that you choose. Sometimes our inability to say no because of our desire to keep our options open or our inability to say yes because of our unwillingness to commit, makes choosing what to wear every day an obstacle by itself. Whether you wear red, blue, brown, or black boils down to a series of yes and no decisions.

To live a purpose-filled life, you need to get into the habit of saying "yes" to the decisions that are going to move you along the path of your purpose. You must also learn to say "no" to the decisions that are going to draw you off your path and compromise who you are even if they sound good. Every day I say yes to writing, I say yes to transforming at least one person's life, and I say yes to reading for my personal growth. I believe that doing these things will advance me along my path. My whole life, I have said no to drinking alcohol, drugs, and smoking because I believe that these things will deter me from my path. Keep in mind that what may deter me may not deter you, so our decision-making will always be different. There are some people who have a high tolerance for alcohol and there are some people who shouldn't drink it at all. That comes from knowing yourself, your strengths, and your weaknesses. The encouraging thing to know is that at the end of this book and all throughout life you will have many decisions to make, but only two choices—yes or no.

Beginning with the end in mind, makes decision-making easier because you see the present moment through the lens of your vision. You can see the dots connect as moments of synchronicity occur throughout your life. If you're clear on your purpose and where you want to go, you can measure every decision according to the choice that is a best fit for you. Even still, there will be times when you feel lost, confused, or stuck. In these moments, you may feel alone because it appears that everyone around you is zooming by. In most cases, this isn't true. In our effort to look like we know the right way, we all cover up the reality that we don't know. Sometimes when we get lost, we drive faster in the wrong direction so that we don't look lost when it would be easier to just stop and ask for help. When you're on track, you will intuitively know because you will experience moments of synchronicity as your path reveals itself and aligns with the purpose your Man-you-fact-urer had in mind when it created you. It's like driving to the airport in a foreign city and starting to see the airport signs 5 miles away from the actual airport, assuring you that you're going in the right direction. Signs will appear to help direct you in the form of people, information, and moments of clarity.

There will also be times where you approach **junk-tions (moments in life where the signs seem like junk)**. The signs you see at these junk-tions weren't a part of your plan therefore they appear meaningless because you may not be open to seeing how they connect or get you to where you're trying to go. It's during moments of confusion like these that accidents tend to occur. **Every obstacle and opportunity is placed before you to help align you with your purpose. Obstacles are in your life to test drive you for future hills and valleys or steer you in the right direction.** You have to decipher which purpose a particular obstacle is serving at a given moment so that you can approach each one with the proper **motive (the pure intention behind your movement)** and learn from it.

DAILY IMPLICATIONS OF PURPOSE

Knowing your purpose will tailor your life in many ways, and there are eight areas of your life that your purpose will definitely affect: education, employment, environment, emotions, energy, expenditures, experiences, and entourage.

THE 8 EFFECTS OF PURPOSE

Education	• What schools should I apply to? • What school should I go to? • What should I major and minor in? • What classes should I take for my major and minor? • How much education do I need? • What kind of scholarships are relevant to me? • What else do I need to learn on top of school? • What books, articles, blogs, or magazines should I keep up with?
Employment	• What company should I intern with? • Who should I position myself to work with after school? • How long should I work with them? • What career path in their company should I pursue? • What companies should I keep an eye on? • What additional skills, training, or credentials will I need to succeed?
Environment	• What city should I live? • Who should I live with? • What type of lifestyle will fit me?
Emotions	• Who should I date and how much? • Do I want to get married? If so, when? • Do I want to have kids? If so, when and how many?
Energy	• How should I spend my weekends? • How and who should I spend my time with? • What organizations should I get involved with?
Earnings	• How much money do I want to make? • Who or what do I want to invest in?
Experiences	• What kind of experiences should I look for (i.e. programs, conferences, etc.)? • What events should I go to? • Where should I travel?
Entourage	• Who should I consider true friends? • Who should I associate with? • Who should seek mentorship from?

Each of these facets of life will be affected by your choices and hopefully influenced by your purpose. Over time, your small yes and no decisions will get you to where you're trying to go. For some people, this book was just an affirmation of the direction you're already going. Others know they need a brand new direction. Some people are right where they need to be but unaware that they are already there. Some people have everything they need but simply need to repurpose themselves in a new career that will allow them to be fully expressed. Wherever you are, you are there for a reason. There are no shortcuts on the journey of life. Each experience has its own purpose.

The concept of repurposing implies that you are perfect as you are, however you may be trying to win in the wrong lane. Post-its were originally a failed experiment until they were repurposed. A scientist at 3M was attempting to make a super-strong adhesive but the result was a compound that could only hold up a piece of paper. Everyone saw it as a failure, until he started using them at his desk and realized how useful they were. Now, post-its is a multi-million dollar market simply because a perceived failure was repurposed.

Donald Clifton sums it up best when he said "Could it be that people are not successes or failures but merely individuals in the right or wrong expectation environment?" There is a lot of information asymmetry in the job search process. It's extremely difficult to find jobs that are aligned with your 8 Cylinders of Success. But by sharing who you are from your point of purpose, you can convert those close to you into your career cupids and matchmakers. Some of world's most successful people started down paths that they thought were aligned with their purpose, but had the courage to change lanes along the way and ended up with something better. Gandhi went from being a lawyer to one of great activist to ever live. Arnold Schwarzennegger went from acting to Governor of California. Malcolm X went from criminal to civil rights intellectual. It's never too late and it is not impossible to repurpose or re-brand yourself.

Eckhart Tolle's book, *A New Earth: Awakening Your Life's Purpose* closes with the difference between our inner and outer purpose. The entire book addresses our inner purpose, which is to be present in the moment, while *The 8 Cylinders of Success* is dedicated to helping people identify their outer purpose. I agree with Tolle, that we can only discover our outer purpose by first being our authentic self in each given moment. I recently discovered a philosophy called teleology. Teleology (Greek: telos: end, purpose) is the philosophical study of design and purpose. Teleology states that "form follows function." For example, a teleologist would say that a person has eyes because he has the need of sight (form following function), rather than a person has sight because he has eyes (function following form).

In the process of purposefinding, function would be your inner purpose and form would be your outer purpose. A single function can manifest itself in many forms. Someone may be born with the function or purpose of healing but the form or profession could take a variety of avenues including:

- Doctor = healer of acute pain
- Psychologist = healer of mental pain
- Minister = healer of spiritual pain
- Activist = healer of social pain

This is the choice where people have the most difficulty because the possibilities are infinite. Which form or profession is the best way for me to manifest my function or purpose? Your 8 Cylinders of Success can help you make this decision. For instance, someone who believes in preventative medicine may not choose to be an emergency doctor because emergency medicine rarely addresses the root cause. Or someone who believes in the power of the mind and its ability to create our reality may choose to be a psychologist over an activist because they believe that if the mind doesn't change, the social problems we see will simply recreate themselves. At the end of the day, they are all healers.

There are multiple ways to accomplish a single purpose and your professional path is the best avenue to do so since you will spend so much of your time on it. Ask yourself if your current professional path feels purposeful to you. Read your company's purpose, vision, mission, and values statement and ask yourself do they align with who you want to be. It's never too late to change your form or profession as long as it is getting you more aligned with your function or purpose.

Sometimes these steps are necessary. Avoiding steps means skipping lessons that come to pass later on, like in the mid-life crisis. Why wait until mid-life to do this introspection when the quarter-life crisis is right before you. Hold off on the house, new car, kids, and anything else that increases your cost of living. Some of these things actually trap people in continuing to do what they hate. By keeping it simple and delaying, you buy yourself time and remain free and flexible to find what you want while someone on society's schedule will being trying to keep up with everyone else by pursuing parenthood and property before purpose. **Who says that you should be married with a house, car, kids, and a million dollars by age 35?** It's another arbitrary number that has no significance. Once you align yourself and begin building a career you care about, then feel free to get all of those things knowing first and foremost that you're on a path you love.

You're never lost on the journey. You're only lost if you're not on the journey. On the journey is where you belong; always changing, growing, and evolving with life. American novelist, Richard Stine, put it best when he said, "I am exactly where I should be, doing exactly what I should be doing...otherwise I would be somewhere else, doing something else." Like improvisation, life is in the moment. As we improvise, we improve within and improvement within always manifest itself outwardly. No matter where life takes you, you can't escape yourself. Wherever you go, there you are.

CONCLUSION

Purpose is not a destination. It is a way of being. There is no rush to get some place. Instead, we need to slow down to be present here and now. Gandhi said, "There is more to life than increasing its speed." We have to learn to enjoy the journey. Experience is worth more than possessions. We even try to turn experiences into possessions with videos, photos, and souvenirs so that we can hold onto old moments, when in fact it is the actual experience we want to relive. Instead, we should spend our energy trying to create new fulfilling experiences for ourselves and others.

Life is full of braking, going, stopping, and shifting. We get impatient at red lights, fear yellow lights, and speed through greens. The fastest way to advance on the path of purpose is to go stoplight to stoplight. **We all want synchronized lights, but that's not a reality. And if we try to wait until all the lights have turned green, we will end up waiting forever.** Parking meters have limits and for some of us, it is time to get moving. You have been licensed to live and drive your vehicle. Leave early and start living a purpose-filled life today.

The Department of Motivated Vehicles has a mantra we recite when people graduate from the Driving School for Life course. As a new member to our community, we want to share it with you so that you can remember who you are and why you are:

"This is my license to live. It never expires. My manufacturer created me with purpose and power. I choose the vehicle I drive, how I drive it, and where I drive it to. The way I drive is more important than the distance I drive. I am empowered to pave new roads and I take responsibility for any accidents I cause. Mistakes are okay. I am fully insured. When I am lost, I stop to ask for help. When I am found, I help others find their way. Collectively, we expand the map of in-possibility. Through proper maintenance of ourselves and each other, we will reach our destine-nation over time."

You are now licensed to live! Go! I pray that you always take the **high road (the decision that aligns with your highest self)** and that this journey leads you to self, health, and wealth.

Godspeed!

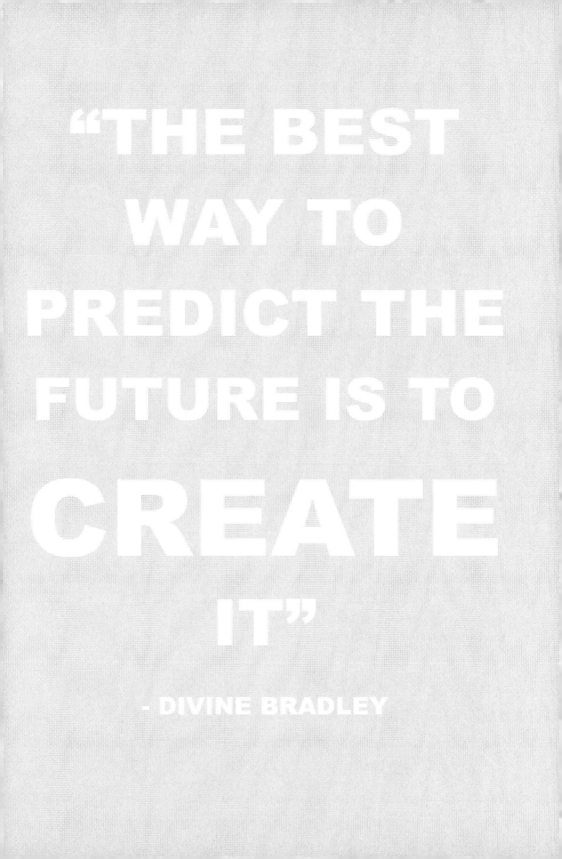

"THE BEST WAY TO PREDICT THE FUTURE IS TO CREATE IT"

- DIVINE BRADLEY

IN-POSSIBILITY

Directions: Complete the following statements for your personal life based on the new possibilities you want to see for the different people you touch with your presence and actions.

Because of my personal life….

…my family will be able to…

....

....

…my friends will be able to…

....

....

…my community will be able to…

....

....

…my world will be able to…

....

....

IN-POSSIBILITY

Directions: Complete the following statements for your professional life based on the new possibilities you want to see for the different people you touch with your presence and actions.

Because of my professional life….

…my customers will be able to…

....

....

…my company will be able to…

....

....

…my colleagues will be able to…

....

....

…my industry will be able to…

....

....

MOVE-MEANT

Where The Rubber Meets The Road

Below are specific actions you can do in the next 30 days to align your life a little bit more with the possibilities you want to create with your personal and professional life.

Personal: Share each of your possibilities statements with someone who fits in the associated category. It's best to share it in-person, but you can also share it via phone, mail, email, website, or blog. Simply observe what kind of energy returns to you from sharing your hope for others.

Professional: Share each of your possibilities statements with your customers, company, and colleagues. It's best to share it in-person, but you can also share it via phone, mail, email, website, or blog. Simply observe what kind of energy returns to you from sharing your hope for others.

ARE YOU
KEEPING
MAPMAKERS
IN
BUSINESS
?

MY ENDING PURPOSE STATEMENT

Directions: Now that you've finished reading the book and have a bit more clarity on your 8 Cylinders of Success, write your new purpose statement using keywords and phrases from your worksheets. You can use the purpose statement template provided below or write it in free form. When you're done, compare it to your first purpose statement and see if you hear or feel a difference.

As of ...., ..., 20.........
          Month   Date   Year

FREE FORM PURPOSE STATEMENT

My purpose is to ....

....

....

....

....

....

....

....

PURPOSE STATEMENT TEMPLATE

My purpose is to extend the possibility of................................

....

to people who...

....

primarily through my passions for....................................

....

Guided by the principles...

....
I focus on creating solutions that address the problems of

....

I picture a life where...

....,

therefore, I observe pioneers such as.............................

....

to position myself to be the best....................................

....

"ALL THOUGH WE'VE COME, TO THE END OF THE ROAD..."

- BOYZ II MEN

NEW LANE-GUAGE

Account-ability = accounting for what we know we have the ability to do

A-line-meant = a state when all of your 8 Cylinders are harmoniously working together for good

Alter-native = a new way that differs from the status quo

Care-er = a profession you care about

Department of Motivated Vehicles = the parent company (i.e. school or university) of Driving School for Life

Destine-nation = your unique end goal, state, or place

Dis-cover = uncovering that which is already within you

Ego-als = lofty goals that sound fly like eagles but are primarily ego-driven

E-motions = emotional energy

En-title-meant = feeling deserving of a title without putting in the required effort to earn it

Entrepre-new-real = imaginative ability to create new realities **Entrepre-new-ers** = those creating new realities through a new organization

Ex-speed-ient = quickly capitalizing on purposeful opportunities

Frame-work = the foundation of beliefs we build our lives upon

Godspeed = a wish for a prosperous journey, success, and good fortune. Our version sincerely.

High Road = the decision that aligns with your highest self

I-dent-ity = an authentic way of living that inevitably shapes the world because of its authenticity
Imagine-nation = the vision you believe is possible
Inter-viewing = the exchange of information between an individual and a company to see if there is interest
Inner-viewing = the process of assessing one's passions, strengths, and fit for a position prior to any inter-view
In-possibility = the belief that anything is possible
In-sights = glimpses of the greatness within us
In the driver's seat = actively participating and present
Intrapre-new-ers = those creating new realities within an existing organization

Junk-tions = intersections in life where the signs seem meaningless like junk

Life-jack = to steal a life

Main-tenets = the inspection of our beliefs or tenets
Man-you-fact-urer = the source that you believe is responsible for your creation
Mechanics = skills and the patterns and routines that support them
Motivated Vehicles = anyone who has gone through the 8 Cylinders of Success
Motive = the pure intention behind your movement
Motor-vator = a person who motivates you on your journey
Move-meant = movement with a particular intention

Net-working = 1. working to increase your net worth 2. casting your opportunity net wider

Officers = people who want security in an office for you over a-line-meant with your purpose

Opti-midsts = hopeful people who are able to see through the midst of uncertainty

Pacesetters = people who you choose to follow and respect for their character and creations
Personal Velocity = the speed in which you are able to get to where you want to go
Pioneers = people who you choose to follow
Pre-serve = to self-inspect and take care of self first
Professional Velocity = your ability to close the distance between point A and B for other people and organizations
Purpose-filled = full of purpose' and meaning

Quest-ions = problem so big that we must go on a quest to find the solution

Red lights = 1. fears that are stopping you 2. things you need to stop doing
Repurpose = to change purpose or function without changing form
Re-tire-meant = an opportunity meant to renew yourself and your goals like you renew your tires; ending one journey or road trip
Roadblocks = problems inside or outside of you that slow your progress
Route-ine = a set of daily, weekly, or monthly actions to maintain progress

Self-expressed = when you a living at your highest personal velocity
Soul-utions = solutions that affect people from the inside out versus the outside in
Street smart = a term often used juxtapose to "book smart" to convey one's level of common sense and understanding

of life regardless of their level of formal education

S.T.O.P. = stillness to observe patterns

Term-oil = things that cause you to slip during a term or period of life

Underemployment = the state of employment where an individual is working below their potential because they aren't passionate about the work or their employer doesn't bring out the best in them by allowing them to play to their strengths

Yellow lights = situations that you approach cautiously

Well-thy = wellness in all areas of life (spiritual, financial, relationships, etc)

ACKNOWLEDGMENTS

Early Editors

Toni Daniels, Tanisha Drummer, Ayinde Jean-Baptiste, Leslie Garner, Sophia Kozak, Boris Kerzner, Danya Steele, Scott Sherman, Vera Moore, Shaquita Murphy, Aimee Slater, Sarah Kolker, Samuel C. Wilson Esq., Sallome Hralima, Wesley Mapes

Book Proposal Reviewers

Keith Andrews, Arcelie Reyes, Daniel Davila, Selome Araya, Manuel Mora, Leslie Garner, Scott Sherman

Marketing

Rolando Brown, Michael Cordero, James Bartlett, Sallome Hralima, Ashley Mui

Family

The Daniels Family, The Gordon Family, The Kelly Family, The Ash Family, The Ikharo Family, The Hopkins Family, The Primas Family, The Chambers Family, The Brown Family, The Shields Family

Mentors

Chip Anderson, Tim Ngubeni, Janet Brown, Andy Chan, Mandla Kayise, Father Malo, Luigi Santini, Reverend Meri Ka Ra, Tom Adams, Michelle Jordan

Companies & Organizations

The 30 Summit, Alcoholics Anonymous, Babe Ruth Baseball League, Be Global, Beginning with Children Foundation, Bishop O'Dowd High School, Charity Focus, The East Bay Church of Religious Science, Educate!, Families for Children, The Gathering, KRST Unity Center, Lakeshore Avenue Baptist Church, Landmark Education, Management Leadership for Tomorrow, MVMT, Mylinia, The National Society of Collegiate Scholars, New York Needs You, Oakland Soccer Club, Plan-It Brooklyn, Potluck International, Real Talk, Sacred Center New York, Spark, Stanford University, Stay Inspired, The Stoop, Transformative Action Institute, UCLA, The UCLA Community Programs Office, The UCLA S.H.A.P.E. Program, Woodworks Records

And all of my friends, readers, and Driving School for Life Alumni

BIBLIOGRAPHY

Books

Buckingham, Marcus. Go Put Your Strengths To Work: 6 Powerful Steps to Achieve Outstanding Performance. New York, NY. Free Press, 2007.

Clifton, Donald O., and Edward "Chip" Anderson. StrengthsQuest: Discover and Develop Your Strengths in Academics, Career, and Beyond 2ed Edition NO CD. New York, NY: Gallup Press, 2006

Clifton, Donald O., and Paula Nelson. Soar With Your Strengths. New York, NY: Dell Publishing, 1992.

Csikzentmihalyi, Mihaly. Flow: The Psychology of Optimal Experience. New York, NY: HarperCollins, 1990.

Damon, William: The Path To Purpose: How Young People Find Their Calling in Life. New York, NY: Free Press, 2009.

Friedman, Thomas. The World Is Flat: A Brief History of the Twenty-First Century. New York, NY: Farrar. Straust and Giroux, 2006.

Gladwell, Malcolm. Outliers: The Story of Success. New York, NY: Little, Brown and Company, 2008.

Godin, Seth. The Dip: A Little Book That Teaches You When to Quit (and When to Stick). New York, NY: Penguin Group, 2007.

Morgan, Adam. Eating the Big Fish: How Challenger Brands Can Compete Against Brand Leaders. New York, NY: Wiley, 2009.

Porras, Jerry I., Stewart Emery and Mark Thompson. Success Built To Last: Creating A Life That Matters. New York, NY: Penguin Group, 2007.The Source

Rath, Tom. StrengthsFinder 2.0: A New and Ugraded Edition of the Online Test from Gallup's Now Discover Your Strengths. New York, NY: Gallup Press, 2007

Tolle, Eckhart. A New Earth: Awakening Your Life's Purpose. New York, NY: Penguin, 2008.

Holy Bible, New International Version, NIV. New York, NY: Zondervan, 2008.

Websites

"76,000 new job cuts announced worldwide." Online. Copyright. January 26, 2009.
<http://blog.cleveland.com/business/2009/01/72500_new_job_cuts_announced_w.html>

"All Time Top 1000 Grossing Films (US)." Online. Copyright

1995-2009. February 12, 2009.
<http://www.movieweb.com/movies/boxoffice/alltime.php>

"Apple customer satisfaction scores gain." Online. Copyright 2008. August 18, 2008.
<http://news.cnet.com/8301-13579_3-10019711-37.html>

"Corporate Information - Our Philosophy." Online. Copyright 2009. November 5, 2008. <http://www.google.com/corporate/tenthings.html>

"Madonna Tops 2009 Music Money Makers List." Online. Copyright 2009. February 12, 2009.
<http://www.billboard.com/news/madonna-tops-2009-music-money-makers-list-1003940730.story>

"Netflix vs. Blockbuster: which one is better?" Online. Copyright 2009. March 23, 2009.
<http://reviews.cnet.com/4520-11445_7-6325775-1.html>

"Patagonia Company Information: Our Reason for Being = Values, Mission Statement." Online. Copyright 2009. March 30, 2009.
<http://www.patagonia.com/web/su/patagonia.go?sc=en_US@sct=US&assetid=2047>

"Potbelly Sandwich Works | Our Story." Online. Copyright 2009. March 16, 2009.
<http://www.potbelly.com/Story/OurStory.aspx>

"Problems at the Top — Apathy, Contempt for Managers."
Online. Copyright 2009. March 3, 2009.

< http://www2.prnewswire.com/cgi-bin/stories.pl?
ACCT=109&STORY=/www/story/
01-21-2005/0002869774&EDATE=>

"Shift Happens." Online. Copyright 2009. January 23, 2009.

<http://shifthappens.wikispaces.com>

"The lonely passion of Will Smith." Online. Copyright 2009.
February 3, 2009.

<http://www.straight.com/node/124495>

"The Millennials: Americans Born 1977 to 1994, 4th ed."
Online. Copyright 2009. July 1, 2009.

<http://www.marketresearch.com/product/displa.asp?
productid=2392602>

"Text of Steve Job's Commencement Address (2005)."
Online. Copyright 2005. June 12, 2005.

<http://news-service.stanford.edu/news/2005/june15/
jobs-061505.html>

"Zappos Core Values." Online. Copyright 2009. February 1,
2009.

<http://about.zappos.com/our-unique-culture/zappos-core-
values>

Videos

"Diddy Blog #7: Diddy & Lil Wane Give Secrets To Success."
Online. Copyright 2008. June 23, 2008.
<http://www.youtube.com/watch?v=3Z80khGVcyU>

"Steve Irwin Before His Death (How He Wanted To Be
Remembered)." Online. Copyright 2006. September 15,
2006.
<http://www.youtube.com/watch?v=yZVPbZ4cKg>

"John & Reve Walsh Speak." Online. Copyright 2008.
December 17, 2008.
<http://www.youtube.com/watch?v=FJckba-TGXO>

News Papers & Magazines

Miguel Helft. "It Pays to Have Pals in Silicon Valley." The
New York Times. October 17, 2006.
<http://www.nytimes.com/2006/10/17/technology/
17paypal.html?pagewanted=print>

Nan Robertson. "Donahue vs. Winfrey: A Clash of Talk
Titans." The New York Times. February 1, 1988.
<http://www.nytimes.com/1988/02/01/arts/donahue-vs-
winfrey-a-clash-of-talk-titans.html>

Richard Zoglin. "Lady with a Calling." Time Magazine. June 24, 2001.
<http://www.time.com/time/magazine/article/0,9171,149830,00.html>

Movies & Music

An Inconvenient Truth. Davis Guggenheim. Video. Paramount, 2006.

Carter, Dwayne, and Sean Carter. "Mr. Carter." Tha Carter III. CD. Cash Money, 2008.

Cook, Charlie. Insider Secrets To 15 Second Marketing. 2007.